A RELATIONAL REALIST VISION FOR EDUCATION POLICY AND PRACTICE

A Relational Realist Vision for Education Policy and Practice

Basem Adi

https://www.openbookpublishers.com

©2023 Basem Adi

This work is licensed under an Attribution-NonCommercial 4.0 International (CC BY-NC 4.0). This license allows you to share, copy, distribute and transmit the text; to adapt the text for non-commercial purposes of the text providing attribution is made to the authors (but not in any way that suggests that they endorse you or your use of the work). Attribution should include the following information:

Basem Adi, *A Relational Realist Vision for Education Policy and Practice*. Cambridge, UK: Open Book Publishers, 2023, https://doi.org/10.11647/OBP.0327

Further details about the CC BY-NC license are available at
http://creativecommons.org/licenses/by-nc/4.0/

Copyright and permissions for the reuse of many of the images included in this publication differ from the above. This information is provided in the captions and in the list of illustrations. Every effort has been made to identify and contact copyright holders and any omission or error will be corrected if notification is made to the publisher.

All external links were active at the time of publication unless otherwise stated and have been archived via the Internet Archive Wayback Machine at https://archive.org/web

Any digital material and resources associated with this volume will be available at https://doi. org/10.11647/OBP.0327#resources

ISBN Paperback: 978-1-80064-898-2

ISBN Hardback: 978-1-80064-899-9

ISBN Digital (PDF): 978-1-80064-900-2

ISBN Digital ebook (EPUB): 978-1-80064-901-9

ISBN XML: 978-1-80064-903-3

ISBN HTML: 978-1-80064-904-0

DOI: 10.11647/OBP.0327

Cover image: Tamanna Rumee, Yellow color pencil isolated on blue paper background (2020), https://unsplash.com/photos/FtJEat_S7Q4

Cover design: Jeevanjot Kaur Nagpal

Contents

List of Figures	vii
Introduction	1
1. The Functionalist Symbolic Reference of UK Governance Models	11
2. Relational Realism as an Alternative General Sociological Approach	43
3. The Morphogenetic Paradigm: Conceptualising the Human in the Social	61
4. Social Capitalisation & the Making of Relational Goods	85
5. Student Development as the Referential Reality of Education	105
6. Morphogenetic Education with a Developmental Mission	121
7. A Summary of the Argument Presented	143
Glossary of Key Terms	155
References	167
Index	179

List of Figures

Fig. 1 For relational sociology, critical realism is an approach that extends the epistemic triangle (Donati 2011: 100). The diagram is adapted to show the epistemic quadrangle in the context of social interventions generating transformational social realities.   54

Fig. 2 The components of sociology as a knowledge system built upon two axes, L–G and A–I (Donati 2011: 105).   56

Fig. 3 Realism's account of the development of the stratified human being (Archer 2000: 260). The diagram is adapted to relational realism and the morphogenetic paradigm.   71

Fig. 4 The emergence of personal and social identity (Archer 2000: 296).   72

Fig. 5 Added social value of sociability (SY) as the re-generation of relational goods (RG) over time (cycle T1–T4), that is, as alteration of the order of relations through the order of interactions (Donati & Archer 2015: 309).   98

Fig. 6 The basic morphogenetic sequence (Archer 2011: 62)..   99

Fig. 7 The components of social relations according to the AGIL scheme (Donati 2011: 87). The diagram has been adapted to show the interchange between the referential (L-I) and organisational (A-G) dimensions of social relations in the context of the morphogenetic emergence of relational goods.   113

Fig. 8 The three-fold view of the curriculum as aspects of different orders of social relationality, adapted from Donati (2021: 56).   123

Introduction

This book presents an argument for a new governance model wherein policy-making is underpinned by a relational realist approach. Its central contention is that prevailing governance models produce analytical closure due to starting from a system-based perspective wherein the state regulates the structure of relations that defines the standards reciprocated between citizens. As a result, the regulation and integration of subjective motivation and its value-orientation represent the central problem of governance. Integration into the state-defined collective becomes necessary to enable the responsible citizen to benefit from public goods and occupy roles contributing to economic growth.

Therefore, a re-think is needed to express responsive modes of sociability that valorise the human element as an active contributor to the production of the *common good*. The position adopted here is that governing bodies benefit from a shift away from providing opportunities in the form of public goods towards the fostering of a relational social state. In the relational social state, individual and collective social actors are *Relational Subjects* who participate in the making of social policies and practices. The starting point for an alternative to state-defined governance is an appreciation of the way these *Relational Subjects* relate to one another in the production of the *common good*. In this book, the idea of a relational social state is applied in the context of education. The student serves as the reference point for identifying the learning criteria that guide the development of agency in potential *Relational Subjects*.

This book builds on key themes in sociological theory, reusing established terminology. When one such term or concept is introduced here, it will be italicised to indicate its inclusion in a glossary at the end of the book.

Why Relational Realism?

In a relational social state, practices and policies emerge from the interdependence of different elements of social relations that generate social structures. Relational realism names an epistemic approach that starts from the ontological reality of these social relations; its explanatory capacity is more encompassing than the self-justifying mechanisms of system-based governance. The nature and benefit of relational realism is perhaps best understood by contrast with contemporary methods of policy formulation and their effects. In late modern social formations, the functionalist conceptual infrastructure is limiting because it oscillates between the state/market binary, thus bypassing the dynamics of social relations.

The current model, against which relational realism is set, is called *lib/lab* governance (Donati 2911; 2021). It works through two poles representing the market/state nexus that forms its operation logic. These poles represent different dimensions of governance. 'Lab' refers to the holism of state interventions that enable individuals to pursue their set of preferences as consumers and producers within a productive economic order. The 'lib' pole, with which it is in continuous tension, encompasses the economic activity of subjects as both producers and consumers and is the referential point of adaptation (Donati 2021). In turn, the state is represented as an organisational dimension that regulates relations to ensure the referential dimension of governance operates to provide opportunities for the individual to occupy roles in the market of goods and services. The referential character of the market (lib) directs the organisational role of the state (lab) and generates modes of observation, diagnosis and intervention that rely on impersonal mechanisms. As will be discussed in Chapter One, the perspective of the subject and the reality of the interactions they stimulate are secondary to the impersonal gaze of the lib pole that represents the finalism of state-defined relations (lab). Hence, the *lib/lab* mode of governance is first an epistemic approach to seeing the world through the prism of the lib end of governance. It sees freedom in a negative sense (freedom *from*), and the referential role of marketisation and economic growth generates inherent tensions that the lab pole needs to adapt continuously. The central goal of the state in the provision of public goods is to ensure fairness that provides access to the same forces of marketisation. By bypassing the dynamics of social relations, both poles become antagonistic, which requires state management. In the case of policy triangulation, as discussed in Chapter One, the attempt to resolve the relationship between both poles through some form of synergy is firmly located within the needs of a productive economic order.

In this book, the need for relational realism is first justified by its conceptual starting point that transcends the functionalist conceptual infrastructure of modernity's *lib/lab* governance. Relational realism is a general knowledge assumption that underpins a mode of observation that explains the relational emergence of the human-in-the-social. This observation is focused not merely on regulating individual preferences but on active mediations that impact the concerns of the observed. The ontological status of mediation between the subject-observer and the object observed in their relationality is the epistemic focus of relational realism and offers insight into the observed object, be that society or a policy of governance.

Rather than impersonal mechanisms steering relations in the *lib/lab* model, the dynamic relationship between observer and observed in relational realism is ascribed an ontological status with a mode of reflexivity that is shaped by the socio-cultural context. Three perspectives are considered in these mediations — the personal, interpersonal, and systemic — as part of a stratified understanding of social reality. To meet the needs of the human individual's constitutive relationality, it becomes necessary to re-draw the epistemic parameters so that social practices organise the structural dynamic that connects freedom and control as part of the dialectic processes of personal and social morphogenesis (covered in Chapters Three, Four, Five, and Six). The necessity of control in relations — the structure that gives purpose and direction — is viewed as emergent from the relationship between observer and observed.

This stratified social ontology, with its concomitant forms of reflexivity, implicates a relational state with a societal governance that encompasses the elements of relations (personal, interpersonal, and systemic). The social includes a relational continuum that comprises personal and collective *Relational Subjects* that operate within a morphogenetic sociocultural context. In turn, within societal governance, the control of the structures of the socio-cultural context is meant to enable positive freedom in the form of *relational reflexivity* capable of transforming the same socio-cultural context in future *morphogenetic cycles*. Freedom is thus understood positively, that is, the capability to act upon the direction of existing mechanisms and their emergent impact on future social relations are recognised. Relational realism understands freedom and control as two interrelated realities that require each other to operate to maintain societal governance and the production of *relational goods* that sustain this governance.

This acknowledgement of the interrelated realities of freedom and control distinguishes relational realism as a general approach and its explanatory powers. To transcend modernity's analytical closure, the societal mode of production necessitates a dynamic that ascribes efficacy to the relationality of the mechanisms of freedom and control. Affirming the societal dynamic between freedom and control is grounded in a *philosophical ontology* that does not dictate the parameters of knowability as it does not establish an *a priori* judgement on the relation's *symbolic reference*. While it starts from the relational constitution of the subject, it does not view this relationality as an end — its realism is identified in its affirmation of the relation and its determinants as co-principles of reality (Donati 2021). Acknowledging determinants in a stratified social ontology means confirming the human and non-human distinction.

The *relational reflexivity* that steers the interdependence between freedom and control entails *relational goods* produced in the third space between freedom (lib) and state-regulated constraint (lab) (Donati 2021). Starting from the relationality of relations results in an approach that avoids the closure of system-based governance while not falling into a relationism that negates the distinctions of pre-existing determinants of sociability. In the context of societal governance, the morphogenesis of both realities of freedom and control ensures *relational goods* generate *Relational Subjects* (engines of morphogenesis) within an adaptable socio-cultural context (constraint). When the subject's identity within the social is acknowledged, the latter can be continuously reimagined in reference to the emergent human reality that pre-exists but is also relationally constituted.

Structure of this Book

Arguing for the necessity of transcending *lib/lab* governance, the book is structured into seven chapters. Chapter One aims to demonstrate the continuity of policy from New Labour to Conservative governments in recent decades. Policy triangulation or a 'third way' is presented as an alternative to the inadequacies of past policy templates in their over-reliance on one pole in governance. The goal is to rectify these limitations by synergising individual freedom (lib) and the state's collective control (lab) within the conceptual infrastructure of a functionalist mode of governance. In the *lib/lab* mode, the attempt to balance individual freedoms and state-defined collective initiatives is defined from the perspective of system needs. The aim is to provide enough space for individuals to identify their needs but always within a regulated environment, which provides the basis for agreed-upon reciprocal interchanges. The relational autonomy of the personality system is pre-defined in the context of a system-based structured dialectic of freedom (lib) and control (lab). In functionalist terminology, the lib side represents the capability of the individual to freely choose a status-role, while the lab side represents the extrinsic powers of the state to intervene to ensure fairness through the provision of opportunities that enable individuals to pursue their choices. Nevertheless, as the attempt to reach a synergy is pre-defined, the horizons of possibility are restricted to maintaining what is posited as adaptations necessary for economic productivity. The freedom to choose a role, therefore, is externally controlled by the state's articulation of the parameters of public goods through which these roles can be accessed.

Chapter Two proposes an alternative epistemic approach capable of opening new horizons that transcend the pre-defined outcomes of system-based governance. First, the chapter argues that an *a priori* epistemic approach is a reasoned necessity. Second, it presents a general approach based on Donati's (2011; 2021) relational realism that takes as its fundamental starting point the relation and its contingencies (the contingencies of social reality being the conditions of emergence of personhood). An epistemic quadrangle is introduced as a map to analyse progressive problem-solving between the observer and observed within the context of mediations between both realities. Mediating these realities establishes a morphogenetic dialectic between lib (freedom) and lab (directive control). Within the morphogenetic dialectic, the person is emergent, raising ethical questions about the human element as an outcome of freedom and control. Because interventions are sought within the mediations, horizons are, by implication, always reflexive and open to novel policies and practices responsive to the human element. Chapter Three, following this implication, expounds on the *morphogenetic paradigm* derived from relational realism.

In the third chapter, the relational realist approach is applied to explain personal morphogenesis. Archer's *morphogenetic paradigm* is expounded as a theory that explores the internal dynamics of relational orders to explain the emergence of the human-in-the-social (Archer 2000; 2003). Derived from the relational realist approach, this paradigm views the deliberations of persons in their relationality. When the mediations are understood as part of relational orders that shape personal concerns, they become the place of interventions to ensure relevance to the human element within socio-cultural contexts. The normative emerges from within the relations that generate reflexive deliberations. Further, the chapter argues that reflexivity as a meaning-making mechanism extends to the personal, collective, and broader social networks — the interactive dynamics of these different facets of sociability anchor social morphogenetic processes. In a relational order of reality, these dynamics valorise the human element as the emergent referential reality of morphogenesis.

Considering policy initiatives, Chapter Four addresses the question of morphogenetic sociability and the making of social capital to generate *relational goods*. The chapter first critiques social capital theories to demonstrate the presence of analytical closure, wherein the dynamics of sociability are viewed as post hoc phenomena. It then presents a contrasting relational view of social capital in which the processes of social capitalisation are disentangled to include the activity of *Relational Subjects* as sovereign actors within a morphogenetic socio-cultural context. The interaction occurs in a relational order (a *civil society*) that *Relational Subjects* mediate between the constitution of sociability and the relational outcomes it produces. In turn, social capital is a crucial relational outcome that enhances the fabric of sociability in future *morphogenetic cycles*. Therefore, social capital is a *relational good*; its features are a process and its outcome is directed by those actively in relation as sovereign producers of a morphogenetic relational order.

The fifth chapter relationally appropriates Parsons's *AGIL scheme* as a compass directed by the morphogenetic developmental points of the learner. The chapter argues that the learner's potentiality is AGIL's value-horizon that orients the structural axis's normative direction. Thus, the integration of the learner into the goals pursued is not regulated from above but is based on the inner dynamics of the relation. While pre-existing learning standards exist as a directive control, they simultaneously enable the development of capabilities. Correspondingly, it will be argued that the dialogical posture of learning is intrinsic to making the structural axis of AGIL responsive to its referential axis, that is, the development of the learner in dialogue with their changing subjective access points.

Chapter Six explores the idea of a relational order of the *civil society* — covered in chapters four and five — in the continuity between different levels of sociability. Specifically, it looks at learning planning within this order when evaluating the student's development as a self-reliant learner and a *Relational Subject*. In teaching and learning, the curriculum is expanded according to the level of sociability to which it refers. Chapter Six thus continues the earlier argument proposed in the book regarding the synergy between sociability's organisational and interactive dimensions. A three-fold distinction will be presented in the curriculum's role as both an aspect of the socio-structural axis of AGIL and as an adaptive resource that references the development of the student (the referential axis of AGIL). In this context, the curriculum is an organisational stabilising mechanism that outlines learning standards which monitor and evaluate learning in immediate relations. In turn, assessment evaluates learning based on criteria pre-set in the delivered curriculum, but *how* assessment strategies are applied first references the developmental point of the learner within the interactive dimension of teaching and learning. The integration of assessment directly into learning re-orients education from a means to sort individuals to take up a status-role to the monitoring and enablement of development as learners and *Relational Subjects*.

Finally, Chapter Seven summarises the argument presented in the book and provides a conceptual guide toward a relational realist view of education. It gives a point-by-point breakdown of each chapter and its relevance to the argument proposed in chapter six of the developmental mission of education.

Immanent Critique

In this book, I will adopt a position of immanent critique when articulating a relational realist alternative mode of governance. First, a transcendental refutation is utilised to establish the underlying pre-suppositions of existing governance models.[1] Based on a transcendental refutation of modernity's *symbolic code* — as covered in chapters one and two — the social effects of governance models are traced to starting points that shape their internal conceptual constitution. Because investigation of the internal *raison d'etre* of a governance approach is pre-supposed by an *a priori* starting point, transcendental critique leads to an immanent critique. A transcendental critique is necessary to identify the starting point of theory articulation that directs its internal logic (Bhaskar 1998).

Immanent critique seeks to show the internal inconsistencies in preliminary premises. Determining how theoretical inconsistencies are reproduced in explanation, an explanatory critique builds on immanent critique as it returns to theory articulation to identify an explanatory logic (the basis of evaluating relations). Finally, the critique of theory application (methodological critique) refers to evaluative claims and the incapability of applying these claims due to internal conceptual inconsistencies (immanent critique).[2]

The immanent critique is applied in Chapters Two, Four, and Five. Chapter Two uses an immanent critique to identify the inconsistencies

---

[1] Transcendental refutation is dependent on transcendental analysis. In transcendental analysis, the conditions of the possibility of social scientific investigation are analysed. Based on this analysis, the refuted account is critiqued in its capability to sustain its premises in reference to these conditions (Bhaskar 1998). In chapter two, the relation as the ontological starting point is justified as being able to sustain itself in reference to the conditions of social scientific activity without leading to analytical closure due to one element being the prism of investigation.

[2] The organic relation between transcendental, immanent, methodological, and explanatory critiques is taken from Bhaskar's metaphysical preliminaries. In these preliminaries, transcendental problems — the way the conditions of possibility of social scientific investigation are defined — generate theoretical, empirical, and methodological problems (Bhaskar 1998: 142).

of both mid-range realism and pragmatist methodological realism. The claims of these approaches — with their differences — show inconsistencies when negating the necessity of an *a priori* starting point and, by implication, the conditions of the possibility of social scientific investigation. Similarly, in Chapter Four, in the case of social capital theory, different starting points identified generate different explanatory outcomes that are incapable of accounting for the process of social capitalisation. Chapter Five, appropriating Parsons's AGIL scheme as a relational realist compass, critiques Parsons's functionalist scheme as incapable of acknowledging the perspective of the human element independent of institutionalised value-patterns. Therefore, the relational realist use of the AGIL scheme becomes a compass to re-direct the referential dimension to the human element.

1. The Functionalist Symbolic Reference of UK Governance Models

In coming chapters, I will argue for a relational approach to governance — with its accompanying mode of knowing — capable of articulating policy initiatives and social practices in ways that acknowledge the human element as a distinct reality. The need for this alternative will be first justified in response to existing approaches to governance in the UK that are conceptually insular. The policies and practices developed in hegemonic governance approaches negate rather than acknowledge relational distinctions; they aim to regulate relations in specific directions to generate outcomes that sustain a pre-given *symbolic reference* with complementary organisational ties. These ties create shared commitments that direct individual subjectivity.

Each social relation has a *symbolic code* that defines its identity (*symbolic reference*) and how its components are integrated. In insular modes of governance, relations are organised to manage differences through pre-existing objectified social formations. Actors are instrumentally encouraged to self-invest, but how they do so depends on the interactions' socio-cultural context. Any distinction in relations (identified in the human element's plurality) is negated through this system-based perspective. Social integration takes a collective dimension that shapes the parameters of exchange between actors and regulates those involved to produce outcomes ensuring an economically productive social order.

In the regulation of individual subjectivity, there is an attempt to balance individuals' liberty as self-maximisers — taking up opportunities to better themselves in guided ways — with a collective sense of belonging to a state-defined national project. Consequently, policy initiatives aim to reach a compromise between self-interested individualism (*homo economicus*) and the need to integrate and regulate this individualism (*homo sociologicus*). The different pathways seeking to achieve this compromise characterise the *lib/lab* mode of governance and its functionalist *symbolic reference*. On the individualist path, the goal is to valorise self-governance as the model of navigating the world. Whereas, on the collectivist path, the state seeks to collectively regulate the environment of interaction to enable individuals to reproduce system needs.

The state-regulated environment means that the state's opportunities (public goods[1]) become a pathway to scarce goods attached to prescribed roles and defined by a competitive situational logic.[2] In this competitive situational logic, the design and application of opportunities guide the acquisition of private goods by providing individuals with tools to make sovereign choices. The end goal in this arrangement is not the development of individuals but the acquisition of system-based accredited goods on a meritocratic playing field.

To demonstrate the centrality of *lib/lab* compromises that shape policy and practice, four UK approaches to governance (derived from New Labour and three Conservative governments) will be discussed:

1. The New Labour approach (1997–2010) sought to regulate social networks through the idea of an enabling state. The state provides

---

[1] Public goods are part of the political system in its setting of collective goals and the allocation of resources (Donati 2011). As a good of the political system, public goods are state-defined (lab) that extrinsically define collective goals. Citizens or collective actors are not sovereign participants in making the relation's 'We-ness' that shapes its direction and value commitments. What differentiates public goods from *relational goods* is that the latter is produced in reconstitutive morphogenetic cycles through the sovereign actions of *Relational Subjects*. *Relational goods*, according to this difference, are part of the referential dimension of the AGIL scheme.

[2] State-provided public goods are strongly tied to providing the means and tools to access opportunities. However, as these opportunities are a bridge to taking up pre-defined roles within relations, they describe the acquisition of private goods that enable individuals to activate their talent. As a result, there is a situational logic in which public goods become the means to sort and credential individuals (credentials being private goods). In the coming chapters, the implications of this situational logic will be seen in assessment planning in which the objective is not the development of all learners but a determination of which individuals are legitimated to succeed.

the tools through which actors responsibly integrate into the collective.

2. The 'Big Society' agenda (2010–2015) sought to remake social networks in pre-given ways.
3. The 'Great Meritocracy' (2016–2019) idea is that the state provides opportunities for individuals to integrate into modes of belonging.
4. 'Unleashing the potential of post-Brexit Britain' (2019–ongoing) combines a renewed civic infrastructure that unleashes opportunities through job-based skills training and broader economic infrastructure investment. Levelling up and providing opportunities leads to greater enterprise and productivity growth.

With differences in focus and approach, each of these four examples points to the same *lib/lab* direction that negates the plurality of the human element by starting from a social integration model that reproduces and sustains system integration in reference to activity within impersonal market mechanisms.

New Labour, Social Networks, and the Enabling State

The New Labour project sought to justify itself by articulating a narrative of change that required specific interventions. These interventions involved the state's re-invention in meeting the needs of a changing world. The imperative of a competitive logic is extended to a global economic order that needs a consensual national society to adapt and work in partnership. As a result, as Morrison observes, a new policy direction was proposed that moved beyond the failures of the Old Left and New Right:

> These are the presupposition, firstly, of a neo-liberal narrative of a changing world that demands adaptation; secondly, of a consensual society that can agree shared values and work in partnership; and, finally, of the failure of both Old Left and the New Right, characterised respectively as the first and second ways, hence the required Third Way (Morrison 2004: 176).

The notion of a consensual society is presented as an alternative mediation to the Old Left's failures and the holism of top-down state provision. To generate an environment that is not centrally regulated, a third way is required that adopts what can be described as 'culture governance' (Donati 2011:206). In this approach, the goal is to empower citizens to be part of the state's provision. Individual conduct becomes part of state-steered partnerships in which self- and co-governance generate the optimal conditions for an economically productive society that is part of a changing world. Culture governance results in a discourse of self-empowerment that is, in reality, self-disciplining:

> Culture governance is about how political authority must increasingly operate through capacities for self- and co-governance and therefore needs to act upon, reform and utilise individual and collective conduct so that it may become amenable to its rule. Culture governance represents a new kind of top-down steering; it is neither hierarchical nor bureaucratic but empowering and self-disciplining (Donati 2011: 206).

New Labour sought to bring about this level of self- and co-governance between state and individual by proposing that norms and values should connect social action — the culture of provision — with a consensual society's institutions. Behavioural changes generate common expectations between provider and recipient. In turn, responsible individuals take up roles that achieve the desired outcomes of sustaining social integration and working partnerships. Worker-citizens claim their stake in a consensual society as part of a mutual duty to improve themselves through the opportunities provided. In the words of Tony Blair, such a society is

> based on a notion of mutual rights and responsibilities, on what is actually a modern notion of social justice — 'something for something'. We accept our duty as a society to give each person a stake in its future. And in return each person accepts responsibility to respond, to work to improve themselves (quoted in Morrison 2004: 114).

The emphasis on co-governance through self-governance — directed via top-down steering — led to subjective and objective formations being part of one process (a theme that recurs in the 'Big Society' agenda). The lab dimension of policy enables this process by producing joined-up networks and investment in supply-side weaknesses at the point of provision (that is, the state connects citizens to networks that provide access to vital public goods). Therefore, this pluralistic and synergistic understanding of provision means co-governance generates a virtuous cycle in which state-steered social networks operate to maintain social integration in times of change and upheaval. According to Tony Blair, it is a method for making a new relationship between citizens and community that is suitable for the 'modern world' (quoted in Morrison 2004: 171).

New Labour's focus on claiming responsibility represented a turn to strategic self-governance that invests in employability. In this model, the self-governing citizen is committed to life-long learning and the development of skills that further the collective project promoted by state-regulated partnerships. Life-long learning is promoted as providing benefits to the individual, to businesses, and to the competitiveness of the national economy:

> All adults need the opportunity to continue to learn throughout their working life, to bring their qualifications up to date and, where necessary, to train for a different job. Now and in the future employability is and will be the best guarantee of employment. Learning also brings broader benefits. It encourages and supports active citizenship, helps communities help themselves, and opens up new opportunities such as the chance to explore art, music and literature. It helps strengthen families and encourages independence. That means that everyone must have access to high quality, relevant learning at a time and pace, and in places that suit them. Not only do individuals, families and communities benefit, learning throughout life also delivers tangible results for business — improved productivity and competitiveness (DfEE 1999: 56).

Thus, New Labour's education policy emphasised learning throughout working life and continuing learning to sustain employability. It linked the enhancement of employability with behavioural outcomes believed to affect collective conduct by strengthening communities and families and improving economic productivity and competitiveness. In these shared mediations of state-steered partnerships, individuals are connected to strategic networks that offer pathways (public goods) to enhance life chances in the long term. Consequently, disadvantage is understood by New Labour as being cut off from a consensual society's norms and values.

In this model of governance, the state's role was to provide opportunities to citizens in the context of the UK's position in a global emerging knowledge economy. The idea of a knowledge economy is the defining feature of a globalised economic order that implicates the necessity of supply-side interventions to remedy skills-gap problems in the workforce. This workforce investment is part of adapting to competitive external conditions between national economies. Skills investment attempts generate advantage through institutional arrangements capable of mediating social pressures represented as natural facts. Thus, for example, New Labour's 'The Future of Higher Education' White Paper (2003) viewed higher education as a global business responsive to the skills demand required for a knowledge-based economy and competitive markets:

> Our competitors see — as we should — that the developing knowledge economy means the need for more, better trained people in the workforce. And higher education is becoming a global business. Our competitors are looking to sell higher education overseas, into the markets we have traditionally seen as ours (DfES 2003: 13).

In the words of Gordon Brown, it is the skills and ability of the workforce that 'define the ability of a national economy to compete' (quoted in Bevir 2005: 113).

The lab's role is to produce institutional arrangements that integrate citizens into broader governance goals. Therefore, objectified institutional arrangements (Bevir 2005: 31) played an essential mediatory role in managing contingencies to ensure the right outcomes were produced. These arrangements become transmission belts between social pressures and envisaged policy outcomes. As a result, in the narrative of social pressures in 'today's world', the right institutional arrangements and policy outcomes are given as natural facts in which initiatives are validated in relation to these same facts (Bevir 2002: 52). What is handed down becomes the collective project of 'one nation'. In a speech to the Confederation of British Industry, Tony Blair stated that all stakeholders contribute to making 'Britain more competitive':

> The choice is: to let change overwhelm us, to resist it or equip ourselves to survive and prosper in it. The first leads to a fragmented society. The second is pointless and futile, trying to keep the clock from turning. The only way is surely to analyse the challenge of change and to meet it. When I talk of a third way — between the old-style intervention of the old left and the *laissez-faire* of the new right —I do not mean a soggy compromise in the middle. I mean avowing there is a role for government, for teamwork and partnership. But it must be a role for today's world.

Not about picking winners, state subsidies, heavy regulation; but about education, infrastructure, promoting investment, helping small business and entrepreneurs and fairness. To make Britain more competitive, better at generating wealth, but do it on a basis that serves the needs of the whole nation — one nation. This is a policy that is unashamedly long-termist. Competing on quality can't be done by government alone. The whole nation must put its shoulder to the wheel (quoted in Fairclough 2000: 26).

Social Capital Investment and Communitarian Themes: Long-Term Investment to Manage Social Pressures and Produce Pre-Set Outcomes

The long-term lab agenda of networked partnerships led to a focus on communitarian and social capital themes. New Labour's turn to co-governance (pluralistic modes of provision) was part of a discourse of empowering local and mid-level collective actors. Innovative modes of state provision were part of an integrative approach needed to manage social pressures in a changing world. Investing in the social is an investment in alternative organisational ecologies and subjective identities. These dimensions — alternative organisational ecologies and subjective identities — are aspects of social investment guided by the state and part of the devolvement of power and responsibility to empower individuals and communities. As such, they are examples of culture governance. Enriching social capital was central to a third way of thinking as an antidote to neoliberalism and the dependency culture of welfarist collectivism: 'Within third way discourses, social capital is presented as an antidote to both socially destructive nature of rampant neoliberalism and the 'dependency culture' produced by excessive collectivism' (Gewirtz et al. 2005: 653).

New Labour's investment in the social as a corrective measure, observed in the adoption of social capital theory and communitarian themes, aimed to tackle possible moral anomie and social fragmentation that arises with unfettered markets (Driver & Martell 1997). Devolution of provision to regional and local social networks sought to transform corporate actors' behaviour and social practices through government recalibration of social networks (Franklin 2007).[3] In the context of a centrally regulated co-governance model, social capital theory is utilised to redefine idealised sources that impact social network outcomes. An affinity is identifiable in Putnam's view of social capital as a self-sustaining virtuous cycle, i.e., networks of families and communities whose relations are enhanced by sources of social capital (features of social organisation). Sources of social capital include 'networks, norms, and trust, that facilitate action and cooperation for mutual benefit' (Putnam, quoted in Portes 1998: 18). Societies rich in the right sources of social capital are better equipped to cultivate desired forms of behaviour that, cyclically, enrich the stock of social capital.

In turn, societies rich in social capital are better equipped to overcome possible structural strains (the social pressures of a changing world) to generate outcomes that advance economic performance and system-wide integration. Reliance on the right sources of social capital — a resource for the dual purposes of ordered social space and economic resource (Franklin 2007) — was part of New Labour's view of the social world as a consensual and ordered space. In this consensual space, policy initiatives work from an unproblematic understanding of what makes for positive system integration. Investment in social capital guides individuals to identify with the normative sources and expectations of social networks. Individuals' integration, achieved through responsible investment in social capital sources, produces a knock-on effect in behavioural changes. The result of managing social pressures and

---

3   To regulate individual behaviour, New Labour adopted practices to produce pre-set outcomes. One example was a reliance on technologies of governance — an ethos of managerialism that measures outputs. In the context of apparent devolution, technologies of governance through numbers became a means to mediate social pressures. Reforms were introduced to cultivate idealised subjectivities (organisational identities) motivated to embrace changes in the way they work. As a result, this meant the need to quantify workplace performance to meet policy outcomes defined by centralised governance goals (Ball 2009). In this context, reforms became a meta-policy status that 'subsumes almost every aspect of public services under its rubric' (Ball 2007: 93). Disciplinary techniques adopted to regulate institutional arrangements included utilising a discourse of contractual obligation for both providers and recipients of services (Fairclough 2000). In the case of providers, for example, in exchange for a pay increase, teachers and nurses, in the words of Tony Blair, were expected in return to 'be prepared to embrace fundamental reform in the way they work' (quoted in Fairclough 2000: 39).

structural strains is individual changes that lead to effective access to strategic networks and opportunities (bridging social capital).

According to New Labour, the community represented a contingent achievement of people acting ethically in fulfilling their duties to others (Bevir 2005: 77). Driver & Martell (1997) consider New Labour's communitarian thinking to place the individual, as a moral and responsible citizen, within a virtuous cycle that generates social cohesion and contributes to the creation of a more viable market economy:

> In Labour's communitarian thinking three themes — economic efficiency, social cohesion and morality — are interwoven. Economic success — particularly more jobs — will bring greater social cohesion, which is further strengthened by a more dutiful and responsible citizenry, and more social cohesion will in turn help create a more viable market economy (Driver & Martell 1997: 34).

As social exclusion is multi-dimensional, re-distributive measures were promoted to tackle the different facets of deprivation, including unemployment, high crime, substandard education performance, and limited aspiration (Levitas 2005). A networked approach to behavioural changes improves employability chances and makes Britain more economically competitive in a changing world (Levitas 2005: 206–209; Fairclough 2000: 57).

Accordingly, New Labour's commitment to communitarian themes was a vital component of a networked society, a bedrock of ties and relationships of trust, values, beliefs, and norms that are all core components of social capital. Communities, as the bonding and bridging social capital, contribute to making ethical and cooperative citizens. Such citizens who fulfil their responsibilities make the most of the opportunities provided by the state and broader social structures. In claiming their stake, they thus realise and demonstrate values within their community and wider society: there is a renewal of civic life in fulfilling responsibilities to others.

Furthermore, New Labour's communitarian thinking, in emphasising the fulfilment of responsibilities, acknowledges a moral underclass. Family and community are structures wherein individuals learn to negotiate the boundaries of acceptable conduct. The implication is that the breakdown of family and community bonds leads to a breakdown of law and order. Inherent in the provision of opportunity is a contractual arrangement whereby individuals claim their stake in society. In the words of Tony Blair:

> The breakdown of family and community bonds is intimately linked to the breakdown of law and order. Both family and community rely on notions of mutual respect and duty. It is in the family that we first learn to negotiate the boundaries of acceptable conduct and to recognise that we owe responsibilities to others as well as ourselves. We then build out from that family base to the community and beyond that to society as a whole [...] we do not show our children respect or act responsibly to them if we fail to provide them with the opportunities they need, with a stake in the society in which they live. Equally, we demand that respect and responsibility from them in return (quoted in Fairclough 2000: 42–43).

In New Labour's approach to *lib/lab* governance and its seeking of a third way, multiple discourses can be identified, including the Labour Party's social democratic tradition. Newman recognizes this multiplicity of discourses to emerge when 'old and emergent regimes interact, with different elements of the new and old being packaged and repackaged, producing tensions and dis-junctures as different sets of norms and assumptions are overlaid on each other' (Newman 2001: 26). In a non-linear understanding of policy production, different assumptions and expectations may co-exist in a governance approach (Newman 2001: 30). Therefore, it is possible to identify different and sometimes contradictory themes within New Labour's policy initiatives as they seek to reach a working *lib/lab* compromise. These themes may co-exist in tension, such as self-governance and open-systems models or policies devolving power to citizens and communities and those preserving centralised governance that sets policy directives from above as an output-based model of managerialism.

The 'Big Society' Agenda: Focusing on Behavioural Adjustments

Integrating individual behaviour through centrally regulated social relations continues in David Cameron's 'Big Society' agenda, first outlined in 2010. However, rather than focusing on regulating top-down social inclusion measures, it focused on managing behaviour by rolling forward local co-governance that stresses social responsibility and initiative. While there are differences in how the *lib/lab* compromise is articulated, there are similarities to New Labour's third way in the vital role ascribed to the social as the site of policy interventions (interventions that are an antidote to transcend past policy failures). In the Big Society agenda, the focus was on localism to enable a more responsive state that empowers individuals and works to generate the conditions of self-dependency. Nevertheless, like New Labour's third way, the citizen's role is viewed in the context of pre-defined system imperatives and the need to make the social work for individuals as members of a national community. From a normative representation, policy initiatives are developed that establish a distinct diagnosis of what went wrong and what may be done to remedy those mistakes.

'Big Society', 'Broken Britain', & Breaking Cycles of Dependency

David Cameron's 'Broken Britain' thesis underlines the normative regulation of social relations through re-worked practices that mediate inter-generational structures. The focus of his 'Big Society' policy response was not merely on making the economy work better for those socially excluded, as was the case with New Labour, but on reversing a moral crisis and bringing coherence to a fragmented normative landscape. Deploying a polemical tone, Cameron presented the welfare state as a harbinger of dependency culture, eroding responsibility and encouraging dispositions that entrap individuals in antithetical life choices and cycles of poverty. He suggested that dependence on local measures, in the form of community and, more importantly, the family, had been compromised by an overbearing big government's nationalisation of social problems. The institutionalization of a welfare system had not rewarded responsibility or granted a voice to citizens, rather, the provision of public services had eroded any notion of responsibility and reciprocity.

'Broken Britain' was a return to New Right discourses on poverty, but Cameron's Conservatives articulated 'the non-financial aspects of poverty' to use them for specific ideological ends. A shift in rhetoric rendered unemployment, for example, a 'structural' problem that created 'perpetual jobseekers', a 'benefits trap', a 'way of life', and the need to replace the conditions that rewarded the work-shy to one in which 'the payment of unemployment benefit by the state is an entitlement which is earned, not owed' (Conservative Party 2009: 12). To counter this 'culture of worklessness and structural unemployment', the party posited a holistic policy that sought to tackle the interconnected paths to poverty, that is, 'family breakdown, serious personal debt, drug and alcohol addiction, failed education, worklessness and dependency' (Social Justice Policy Group 2007: 5). However, 'Broken Britain' was not just a policy of blame with an imperative for individual self-improvement. Instead, it was a stance that, while acknowledging the necessity of 'Thatcherite modernisation', conceded that problems had been generated by its reforms of hyper-individualism to an over-reliance on the centralised power of the state to push ahead with economic reforms (McAnulla 2010: 290).

In the spirit of *lib/lab* policy triangulation, the state — specifically the welfare state — erodes responsibility and entraps individuals into cycles of disadvantage and poverty. Thus, as with New Labour's third way, David Cameron offered the idea of the 'Big Society' as a policy that transcended what is represented as the traditional Left/Right dichotomy:

> The left in politics talk too much about the state. And the Right sometimes talks too much about the individual. But what really matters is what is in between — society (Cameron 2009a).

Connected to the Conservative Party, the think-tank 'The Centre for Social Justice' emphasised this political triangulation in their publication 'From Breakdown Britain to Breakthrough Britain' (2007):

> The traditional 'laissez-faire' approach understands poverty simply as a product of wrong personal choices about family, drugs, crime and schooling. That view says that poverty is always the fault of the person who makes the wrong choices. On the other side of the political divide, the elimination of poverty is seen principally as the job of government — thus if a person is in poverty it must be the government's fault and it must be the government that develops a top-down solution to the problem (Social Justice Policy Group 2007: 7).

In place of the maligned welfare state, the policy called for public services to be provided beyond the state. 'Big Society', in the form of the locale and community, between both state and individual, was viewed as the appropriate site of welfare provision and simultaneously given the role of creating 'avenues through which responsibility and opportunity can develop' (Cameron 2009b). Through a 'radical decentralisation' of power, service recipients would be empowered and inter-generational structural disadvantage would be countered (Cameron 2009c). Rolling back the state would serve to roll forward society and break cycles of dependency and selfish individualism.

By creating the 'Big Society', the government resituated itself as a guide, partner, and instrument in engineering changes to remedy behavioural pathologies. In the words of David Cameron: 'But I see a powerful role for government in helping to engineer that shift. Let me put it more plainly: we must use the state to remake society' (Cameron 2009b).

The 'Big Society' agenda sought to strengthen and encourage social entrepreneurship within local institutions embedded in communities, generating solidarity, and making welfare provision more personal. It advanced the idea that strong local institutions would enable people to come together and work on a responsive provision (Cameron 2009b). As envisioned, individuals would be encouraged to make the right choices by the cultivation of a more responsive service through the devolution of provision. The intended effect of this devolution was a shared responsibility for social welfare, so that provision would become a shared burden and not solely the government's job.

Nudging citizens towards positive choices, whether through devolving powers to communities or introducing tax credits and benefits for families, empowers both communities and families with purpose. New conditions were envisaged to break a cycle of poverty, especially early on in a child's development (Social Justice Policy Group 2007: 8–9), by encouraging aspiration, the take-up of newfound opportunity, and behavioural changes. Ascribing significant importance to a new environment of a public provision meant breaking inherited subjective experiences that come with pre-existing social positionalities, for example, intergenerational worklessness with its subsequent 'state of mind'. To achieve this objective, what was required, according to the Social Justice Policy Group, was the breaking of a 'cycle of disadvantage in the early years of a child's life' by rolling 'forward the frontiers of society by extending the parameters of social responsibility' (2007: 7).

A consistent theme emerges in 'From Breakdown Britain to Breakthrough Britain'— individuals make wrong choices, but policy initiatives cannot regulate individual choices. Thus, the creation of the right structures and environment for individuals and communities would enable self-dependency: 'On the contrary, what we should be doing as politicians is, wherever possible, creating the right structures and environment for individuals and communities to help themselves' (Cameron & Herbert 2008: 123).

With this focus on the right structure and environment, 'From Breakdown Britain to Breakthrough Britain' further describes New Labour's state interventions as piecemeal, to be superseded by a Conservative holistic and structural approach. The mutualism of 'Big Society' offers avenues of opportunity — corrective behavioural measures — through a network of empowered local institutions meeting citizens' needs. Membership in these organisations fosters responsibility and a more accountable and responsive welfare provision.

Like New Labour's co-governance themes, the citizen in the 'Big Society' is a stakeholder in public provision; he or she takes responsibility for its delivery and balances citizens' rights as consumers of these same services. Through taking responsibility, citizens acknowledge their shared responsibility, hold public services accountable, and are incentivised by the government to take up opportunities. The difference between New Labour and the Conservative 'Big Society' approach to triangulation is New Labour's greater focus on initiatives that produce social inclusion. Thus, as noted above, New Labour aimed to connect citizens to the right self-improvement resources through networked interventions that generate behavioural changes. While a moral underclass discourse is implied in this approach, there is no pre-existing assumption of a systemic normative breakdown. Conservative policy under David Cameron, on the other hand, focused on the erosion of responsibility, inculcated by a paternalistic state, which requires an alternative ethos that encourages citizens to adopt a 'collective culture of responsibility' and an 'ethos of self-betterment' (Cameron 2011).

The remaking of society was deemed necessary for a more responsive devolved public service (better provision) and a holistic delivery of these same services. This holistic approach included early-life interventions and paternalistic nudges to guide choice-strategies that sustain and complement the state's enabling role. This assumption of a holistic approach to welfare provision led David Cameron's Conservatives to accuse New Labour's policies of being both piecemeal and insufficient in tackling social exclusion problems. Nonetheless, both approaches maintain a functionalist understanding of social integration but differ in strategies adopted to connect individuals to the general system of social action and its pre-defined goals.

Welfare Co-Production & Redefining State Provision

As social disadvantage is viewed as a structured outcome and the site to develop an ethos of self-responsibility, policy initiatives focus on community development as the means to achieve this goal. The 'Big Society' agenda, as set out by the Community Development Foundation, defined the role of community development as 'empowering communities, opening up public services and promoting social action', and all three mentioned components 'will require greater cooperation and unity among local people, and between local people and the authorities that serve them' (Community Development Foundation 2010: 2).[4] The three components are intertwined; empowering communities will open up public services and promote social action (active citizenship). The third role of community/social action is to offer 'social value and complements or fills gaps in public services' (Community Development Foundation 2010b: 3). These three components thus fulfil two overarching and related objectives: 'localism and redefining the role of the state' (Community Development Foundation 2010b: 3). The state's redefined role is understood as an enabler of welfare co-production, in partnership with local people, and in being responsive to citizens, altering its provision to meet local people's needs.

Two themes may be identified with the above vision of welfare co-production:

1. A process view of service provision indicates a change in the nature of public service delivery. The resulting change leads to a responsive and open state engaged in the service-delivery environment and

---

4 The Community Development Foundation was chosen by the Coalition Government to deliver a £80m programme to help strengthen communities from 2010 to 2015 (Cabinet Office 2011).

the transformation it may generate through this same delivery. Consequently, there is a shift from the delivery of service as targets or outputs defined as 'top-down regulations and targets' to 'bottom-up accountability — individual choice, competition, direct elections and transparency' (Cameron & Clegg 2010).

2. Changing citizen behaviour and outlook by giving communities full responsibility for their lives. A responsive state encourages community action and devolves power to the locale. As a knock-on effect, it implicates a change in the citizen's habitus and the state's efficacy in meeting citizens' needs.

The first theme — a process view of public service provision — aims to respond to consumers' lived expectations in both delivery and outcome. As a result, there is a view of service provision in which 'there is no separation between production and consumption of a service; they happen simultaneously' (Klein 2010: 3). Objective outputs and subjective changes become inseparable, with citizens being transformed as they take responsibility for services in their communities. Subjective transformation necessitates creating 'the right structures and environment for individuals and communities to help themselves' (Cameron & Herbert 2008: 123). Whitaker describes this co-production view as follows:

> In 'delivering' services the agent helps the person being served to make the desired sorts of changes. Whether it is learning new ideas or new skills, acquiring healthier habits, or changing one's outlook on family or society, only the individual served can accomplish the change. He or she is a vital 'co-producer' of any personal transformation that occur. The agent can supply encouragements, suggest options, illustrate techniques, and provide guidance and advice, but the agency alone cannot bring about the change. Rather than an agent presenting a 'finished product' to the citizen, agent and citizen together produce the desired transformation (Whitaker 1980: 240).

Policy initiatives become necessary to establish a process approach to service provision by generating the right structures and environment for individuals and communities to help themselves. For this objective, instruments were set out, including the training of community organisers, to assist in self-help groups' operation and organisation. Both the institutional framework and situational factors (choice context) were viewed as key interventions in generating the right conditions through which 'government can harness the power and potential of self-help to meet the converging ambitions of localism and the Big Society' (Archer & Vanderhoven 2010: 5).

Institutionally, policy initiatives were utilised to devolve powers to the micro-level. In terms of actual policy initiatives, the Conservative Party sought to redefine responsive public service through the following measures:

1. The reduction of bureaucratic and red-tape burden on local community organisations and businesses.

2. The establishment of neighbourhood grants and start-up funds for community groups to generate social capital in the poorest areas.

3. The support of self-help groups, for example, co-ops, mutuals, charities and social enterprises (Conservative Party 2010a & 2010b), as front-line providers of a double devolution of public services (Community Development Foundation 2011).

4. Setting up a national citizen service as 'a two-month summer programme for 16-year-olds' that facilitates community engagement. According to the Conservative Party, this was a longer-term strand of the policy: 'This is about sowing the seeds of the Big Society — and seeing them thrive in the years to come' (Conservative Party 2010b: 2).

5. The designation of a 'Big Society Day' aimed 'to celebrate the work of neighbourhood groups and encourage more people to take part in social action projects' (Conservative Party 2010a: 2).

6. A proposal to set up national centres to train community organisers with the necessary skills and expertise to assist self-help groups in providing localised public services. While not paid, community organisers will 'help communities to establish and operate neighbourhood groups, and help neighbourhood groups to tackle difficult social challenges' (Conservative Party 2010a: 6). Also, intermediary bodies were viewed as a bridge between self-help groups and the successful provision of services that require expertise, skills, and successful mediation between the state and the locale. For this purpose, the Conservative Party envisaged a role for civil servants and trained community organisers, fulfilling the key functions of intermediary groups (Archer & Vanderhoven 2010). Regarding civil servants, the Conservative Party sought to 'transform the civil service into a national "civic service"'. This

> change of ethos was to be enacted 'by making regular community service, particularly in the most deprived areas, a key element in staff appraisals' (Conservative Party 2010a: 7).

The proposal of a more responsive state (as demonstrated in the initiatives noted above) was part of a process to generate citizens' transformation. It works to create an altered terrain conducive to a different and responsible outlook. As a result, welfare co-production is understood as more than an individualised workfare model — a model in which individual rights are preceded by a responsibility to seek out and take up opportunities. While an individualised dimension existed within the 'Big Society' agenda, there was a greater emphasis on the collective in welfare co-production that is preceded, as noted, by a conducive structure and environment. As a processual approach does not focus on the top-down production of set service outputs, the locale's collective assets are sought to generate outcomes that feed into a virtuous cycle of welfare co-production.

Citizen co-production is part of the virtuous cycle in which behavioural changes — maintaining a self-reliant culture — break intergenerational cultures of dependence and sustain self-reliant community groups. Whitaker (1980) categorises three types of citizen co-production; these types recognise a relational inseparability between the citizen and a responsive institutional environment:

> (1) Citizens requesting assistance from public agents; (2) citizens assisting public agents; and (3) citizens and agents interacting to adjust each other's service expectations and actions (Whitaker 1980: 242).

All three categories rhetorically existed in Conservative policy (cf. Cabinet Office: Behavioural Insights Team 2010 & 2011), ranging from open communication on local needs between service providers and citizens, cooperation in the delivery of services (e.g., recycling waste), and finally in the existence of self-help groups as service providers, with the government as an enabler in this process.

Nudging Community Action & Changing the Decision Context

Libertarian Paternalism complements the 'Big Society' policy vision. The Conservatives adopted 'nudge theory' — part of the lab component of governance — to restructure the choice context to generate different social practices and conditions and to cultivate specific subjectivities. With its focus on developing a choice-architecture for self-help groups and individuals, the 'Big Society' approach 'nudged' citizens with a combination of Libertarian Paternalism (Thaler and Sunstein 2003) and Libertarian Welfarism (Korobkin 2009). In these, the consequences of individual choices, as covered above in the case of a virtuous cycle of welfare co-production, are more than a matter of maximising personal utility; they include collective welfare. Because the 'Big Society' vision places sustainable communities at its core, supporting policies seek to go beyond personal behavioural change. Self-help was thus viewed primarily as a collective initiative that provides direction to changes in individual behaviour.

Nudge theory (Libertarian Paternalism) assumes a negative view of human decision-making. Individuals, it is argued, often make decisions that are detrimental to both themselves and the greater public good. In the *homo economicus* view, human nature is characterized by 'unbounded rationality, unbounded willpower, and unbounded selfishness' (Mullainathan & Thaler 2000). Thaler and Sunstein propose the contrasting term *'homer economicus'* to denote that 'people have self-control problems' (Thaler and Sunstein 2003: 176). Self-control problems — bounded willpower and rationality — can include a judgemental bias, status-quo bias, context-dependent preferences (the situational factors of decision-making (Korobkin 2009)), and susceptibility to social influences such as herding (Thaler and Sunstein 2009; Thaler and Sunstein 2003).

To alter the decision-making process, Thaler and Sunstein recommend an array of possible avenues or a toolbox that can nudge the citizen in directions that counter potential problems arising from bounded rationality and willpower. For the provision of such a toolbox to qualify as Libertarian Paternalism, however, coercion must be carefully circumvented, and citizen welfare promoted to render it unobjectionable:

> But since no one is forced to do anything, we think this steering should be considered unobjectionable to libertarians (Thaler & Sunstein 2003: 177).

For example, overcoming a status-quo bias or inertia can be achieved by introducing automatic enrolment for pension schemes that do not coerce the citizen, as it offers a possible opt-out. The setting of such defaults is considered an unavoidable nudge, but other nudges exist that can be deployed to prevent or remedy common errors in decision-making. These include providing feedback and advice. Examples include (Thaler, Sunstein, & Balz 2010):

- Providing a map of welfare provision and explaining public-service choices and what they entail.
- Structuring complex choices to avoid possible confusion and accompanying services with well-thought-out information that enables the user to learn about possible decisions to reach an informed choice.
- Providing incentives for certain choices by making salient the outcomes they produce.

Nudges exist in policies that target individual choices. For example, organ donation, smoking, diet and health problems require the dissemination of information to allow the making of more informed choices. However, in terms of the 'Big Society' agenda, nudge theory was viewed as more than a useful means of cultivating citizen behavioural adjustment. It also extended to what can be described as Libertarian Welfarism, in which interventions or nudges encourage collective well-being through behavioural changes that extend beyond personal benefit. Overall, nudges were envisaged in terms of 'the power of the crowd'; this power is both collective and collaborative, where consumers work 'together for a better deal', which includes 'introducing a range of new initiatives that will support the development of collective purchasing and collaborative consumption' (Cabinet Office: Behavioural Insight Team 2011: 6-7). The collective dimension of the 'power of the crowd' was part of a joint government initiative that advocated government-business-community partnerships based on allocating budgets to the locale at the point of delivery.

The 'Big Society' agenda thus extended Thaler and Sunstein's notion of a nudge-choice architecture to collective enterprises and collaborative efforts. In the previously noted example of community organisers who work with intermediaries to nudge self-help groups to take responsibility for public service provision, nudges could take the form of the dissemination of information via intermediaries and the social structuring of choice mechanisms. Also, incentivising nudges are sought to generate an intrinsic motivation to participate when devolving power, that is, a sense of self-determination and belonging for local services (an envisaged 'Big Society Day' is one such nudge in this direction) (Klein 2010). Other incentives included monetary funding of local self-help groups via a proposed 'Big Society Bank' (Archer & Vanderhoven 2010).

Because the transformation of citizen behaviour is tied to a broader welfare co-production in public service, Conservative policy sought to achieve a more holistic approach by 'facilitating the design and delivery of other services with diverse sector partners' (Cabinet Office: Behavioural Insight Team 2011: 4). In delivering services, this partnership was sought within a three-level ecosystem conception of 'Big Society'. Each level has its designated role — from the government (both central and local) to government partnerships with both private and social sectors and finally to the locale as a point of delivery delivered by both citizens and self-help groups (Cabinet Office: Behavioural Insight Team 2011). Thus, the overall policy objective trickles down, and nudges occur at all levels of the 'Big Society' vision. While David Cameron viewed the state as reconfiguring the social landscape, with paternalistic nudges as a means, the Conservative Party understood this process as a collective and collaborative effort and not a matter for the state alone.

The coordination of social activity became the role of the lab pole of governance. In turn, the lib side would fuse with the lab's social initiatives, in which a pre-diagnosed normative breakdown would be remedied. The individual's subjectivity is contextualised in and through the corrective role of 'Civic Conservatism' (Williams 2019). This approach involves individual behaviour being nudged and guided towards self-responsibility by way of a coordinated shared terrain engineered through state-led partnerships. The stronger focus on a moral underclass discourse, compared to New Labour, resulted in collectivism that hinged on a culture of mutuality in which it was posited that power would be devolved to the locale. Centralised regulation and bureaucracy that, according to David Cameron, exists in the overbearing lab side of governance takes control and responsibility away from citizens to make their social world:

> The paradox at the heart of big government is that by taking power and responsibility away from the individual, it has only served to individuate them. What is seen in principle as an act of social solidarity has in practice led to the greatest atomisation of our society. The once natural bonds that existed between people — of duty and responsibility — have been replaced with the synthetic bonds of the state — regulation and bureaucracy (quoted in Gibson 2015: 41).

The state under 'Big Society' policy did not aim merely to enable access to strategic networks; instead, it sought to engineer new conditions in which co-producing communities could thrive and, as a knock-on effect, access self-betterment resources. By producing the normative foundations of reciprocity, the government would become the bedrock that sustains free markets and grows a competitive national economy.

The 'Great Meritocracy': A Strong and Inclusive Economy

Under the leadership of Theresa May (beginning 2016), Conservative policy continued the trend of policy triangulation. Generally, the 'Big Society' idea persisted in acknowledging a 'shared society' (Williams 2017). However, emerging ideological polarities took a practical turn in what the government might achieve:

> We must reject the ideological templates provided by the socialist left and the libertarian right and instead embrace the mainstream view that recognises the good that government can do (Conservative Party 2017: 7).

The shift to a 'mainstream view' meant that importance was ascribed to taking 'decisions on the basis of what works' and 'what matters to the ordinary, working families of this nation'. Essential to the government's ability to do good, it declared, is a strong economy: For, 'without a strong economy, we cannot guarantee our security, our personal prosperity, our public services, or contented and sustainable communities' (Conservative Party 2017: 6).

The lab side of governance is seen in interventions designed to deliver a more robust economy that works for everyone. Like New Labour, there is no focus on a normative breakdown. Instead, the government acts to remedy the supply-side skills gap and provide access to better-paid jobs. A modern industrial strategy was proposed to deliver a strong and inclusive economy that distributes opportunities fairly and on merit:

> Our modern industrial strategy is designed to deliver a stronger economy that works for everyone — where wealth and opportunity are spread across every community in the United Kingdom, not just the most prosperous places in London and the south-east. It will help young people to develop the skills they need to do the high-paid, high-skilled jobs of the future. And it will back Britain for the long term: creating the conditions where successful businesses can emerge and grow, and helping them to invest in the future of our nation (Conservative Party 2017: 18).

The modern industrial strategy was positioned as central to reducing inequalities between communities. Government investment aimed to generate sustainable and inclusive growth based on a shared distribution of wealth between communities. In this sense, the 'shared society' under Theresa May directed focus onto practical initiatives that would deliver sustainable growth:

> We will use the structural fund money that comes back to the UK following Brexit to create a United Kingdom Shared Prosperity Fund, specifically designed to reduce inequalities between communities across our four nations. The money that is spent will help deliver sustainable, inclusive growth based on our modern industrial strategy (Conservative Party 2017: 35).

Under this plan, work-based welfare was the best means to ensure prosperity, and getting people into work was believed to provide the best route out of poverty. Participation in the workplace was advanced as the practical means for assisting individuals and growing the economy:

> Employment is at a record high and we will continue to strive for full employment. We will continue to run the welfare system in accordance with our belief that work is the best route out of poverty, that work should always pay, and that the system should be fair both to the people in need of support and those who pay for it. We have no plans for further radical welfare reform in this parliament and will continue the roll-out of Universal Credit, to ensure that it always pays to be in work (Conservative Party 2017: 54).

Education was a key facet of the plan. Employers were placed at the centre of proposed reforms to offer 'world-class technical education' developed in partnership with the British industry that addresses skills shortages. Again, continuing the trend of New Labour, lifelong learning and technical education were to be made accessible:

> We will establish funding streams to ensure investment for the long term, and make a modern technical education available to everyone, throughout their lives, to provide the skills they need. We will remove the barriers that hold back small firms with big potential — and let them compete when government itself is the buyer (Conservative Party 2017: 19).

The lib side of policy triangulation emphasises personal effort to make the most of individual talents. Reliance on personal initiative is possible when the government ensures everyone has a chance to advance. When social injustices are tackled — framed primarily in terms of obtaining work-based skills — opportunities emerge that enable individuals to succeed in the defined context of a national industrial strategy. The result was the making of a 'Great Meritocracy' in which hard work would be rewarded and where advantage would be based on merit, not privilege:

> The greatest injustice in Britain today is that your life is still largely determined not by your efforts and talents but by where you come from, who your parents are and what schools you attend. This is wrong. We want to make Britain the world's Great Meritocracy: a country where everyone has a fair chance to go as far as their talent and their hard work will allow, where advantage is based on merit not privilege. To succeed, we must redouble our efforts to ensure that everyone, no matter who they are or where they are from, can have a world-class education (Conservative Party 2017: 49).

The 'Great Meritocracy' idea is closer to New Labour than Cameron's 'Big Society'. It understood the lab role of governance as providing opportunity and the expectation that individuals will contribute to a pre-defined national strategy. Compared to Cameron's 'Big Society', what distinguishes the 'Great Meritocracy' is its emphasis on initiatives based on 'what works' rather than claiming a societal breakdown and inherited states of thinking and living. Social cooperation between the government and employers is the means to provide responsive work-based skills that enable social mobility and self-responsibility.

The Post-Brexit Challenge: Levelling-up Unleashes Opportunities

The move towards reaching a compromise between the *lib/lab* sides of governance continued with Boris Johnson's post-Brexit Conservative government (2019). Because previously Labour-voting constituencies in the north of England turned to the Conservative party, a tactical strategy was devised to maintain this support. A levelling-up approach became the defining policy feature, describing government aims to invest in infrastructure to connect urban centres to achieve and improve mobility between places (Tomancy & Pike 2020).[5] Investment in infrastructure also included investment in education to tackle supply-side weaknesses. In the words of Boris Johnson, the problem was one of supply in which Further Education (FE) colleges were failing to endow their students with relevant skills:

> We are short of skilled construction workers, and skilled mechanics, and skilled engineers, and we are short of hundreds of thousands of IT experts. And it is not as though the market does not require these skills. The market will pay richly. The problem is one of supply — and somehow our post-18 educational system is not working in such a way as to endow people with those skills (Johnson 2020a).

The lab's governance role is to provide opportunities to access necessary training to take up well-paid jobs. This entails focused investment in technical training that produces transferable skills. To enable the lib side to work, the government promised a skills guarantee for individuals to train and retrain at any time in their lives (Johnson 2021a). The proposition responded to changes in the UK economy accelerated by the Covid pandemic by ensuring that individuals would be better positioned to find new and better jobs. Boris Johnson's government, recognising the rapid process of change, put forward investment in infrastructure in the form of science and technology to enhance productivity and growth:

---

5   The objective in transport infrastructure investment is to connect marginalised places to centres of urban growth. The knock-on effect of this investment is furthering social mobility by providing access to skilled and well-paid work (Tomancy & Pike 2020).

> We're making unprecedented investments in infrastructure — and doubling the investment in science and technology from £11 billion to £22 billion a year by 2024 (Johnson 2020a).

Technical education is part of the investment in infrastructure that has the dual purpose of providing opportunities to individuals and adapting the nation to 'build back better' (Johnson 2021a). Similar to New Labour, the idea is to encourage individuals to take up opportunities and, in turn, acquire the necessary skills that generate further productivity and growth. Therefore, investment in the right infrastructure results in a trained workforce that can 'build back better'. Aligned with the levelling-up initiative, the policy direction was to invest across all regions to unleash opportunities and generate the skills the economy needs (Department for Education 2021). Boris Johnson described the increased investment in work-based skills as a 'Fair Deal' that delivers an 'Opportunity Guarantee' (Johnson 2020b).

The dual approach of investment in technical training to generate individual and national opportunities — continuing the policy blueprint of previous Labour and Conservative governments — can be seen in the government's education Whitepaper 'Skills for jobs: Lifelong Learning for opportunity & Growth' (2021). In the report, the government set out its aims to strengthen the link between FE education and employers through active partnerships. Thus, the reform of FE was tied to putting employers at the centre, where education and training lead to jobs that improve productivity and further close the skills gap. In turn, educational institutions are given the autonomy to adapt and develop courses in cooperation with the government and local employers. To enable this process, Boris Johnson's Conservative government proposed a strategic development fund that planned to improve partnerships in which providers would be 'empowered to shape their provision to respond to skills needs' (Department for Education 2021: 18). The state, in this scheme, would regulate post-16 technical and higher education and training to meet employer-led standards. New powers for the secretary of state for education were proposed to allow for direct intervention when providers did not deliver the skills needed by employers:

> Strengthen the governance of colleges, by taking a clearer position on what good governance and leadership looks like and placing specific

requirements on colleges and other provider types... This includes setting out clearer expectations, requirements, and support to empower weaker colleges to address problems earlier, as well as ensuring that college corporations can govern effectively and autonomously (Department for Education 2021: 12–54).

Although Boris Johnson claimed that the boost to vocational education represented a 'radical change', it is, in fact, the same path taken by previous governments. For example, work-based learning under Theresa May's leadership was extended to all aspects of higher education. Accordingly, degrees were expected to include 'significant periods of work experience' so that 'practical experience of the workplace [would] become the norm in degrees and an integral part of making students "work ready"' (Department for Education 2019: 11). Furthermore, under Theresa May, social justice measures to widen participation were similarly set in the context of economic productivity in which opportunities provided required greater institutional accountability on graduate employability outcomes.

Under Boris Johnson's leadership, the Conservative Party did not explicitly argue that society had broken down; yet, it adopted a moralising tone with regard to the preservation of national identity. The use of nationalist rhetoric and signifiers, though influenced by the post-Brexit landscape (Sobolewska & Ford 2020), also supported a broader electoral strategy to gain and keep traditional Labour voting constituencies.[6] In contrast to larger cities, smaller towns and rural areas in the North and Midlands predominantly voted to leave the European Union and led to the intensification of inter-regional polarisation. As Mackinnon (2020) observes, the Brexit referendum's result manifested pre-existing regional inequalities that included New Labour's weakened relationship with its post-industrial working-class regions.

Brexit, therefore, accelerated the momentum of change. In continuity with Theresa May, Boris Johnson specifically targeted leave-voting seats — part of the broader 'levelling-up' agenda — by promising sustainable economic regeneration to communities 'left behind' with the aim to

---

6 This electoral strategy is seen in the 'Town Deals' scheme that disproportionally selected towns for funding — to improve local infrastructure — based on them being marginal Conservative-held parliamentary seats (Hanretty 2021).

deliver long-term economic and productivity growth (Johnson 2019). A fairer distribution of opportunity, thus, was tied to solidifying strategic electoral wins. Through greater and more equitable infrastructure investment, the creation of high-skilled jobs and highly skilled employees would drive the prosperity of previously neglected regions.

While Boris Johnson's Conservative government did not have a broader vision like New Labour or the 'Big Society' agenda, it still maintained the same blueprint of *lib/lab* triangulation. In this blueprint, the government tries to compromise between collective interventions and individual subjectivities that self-invest and sustain a greater state-defined mission. Despite the rhetorical acknowledgement of partnerships, cooperation, and stakeholders, it is a return to a work-based welfare model. Individuals self-invest — provided with tools and opportunities — to become 'work ready' self-responsible citizens. Measures are adopted, for example, through career guidance, to direct personal choices in ways that maximise earning outcomes and provide relevant skills wanted by employers. 'Levelling up' and 'building back better' are part of one virtuous cycle — distributive fairness provides opportunities that generate skills-based outcomes and connect citizens with better jobs, resulting in greater national productivity.

When Devolution is not Devolution

As noted in the introduction, while there are differences, the models of policy triangulation point to attempts to reach a compromise between the *lib/lab* poles of governance. In various ways, the state (the lab pole) is viewed as a partner that ensures opportunities are accessible through investment in non-centralised public service infrastructure. In turn, the lib pole relates to self-responsible individuals who maximise the opportunities provided within a greater state-defined project. The discursive move to devolution, partnerships, and stakeholders is part of an attempt to reform what is presented as the failures of traditional political templates in maintaining system-based integration. Consequently, despite devolution discourse, the relational reciprocity between individuals is appropriated by state-led mutual socialisation to meet the economic needs of a globalised world.

Although claiming to transcend past policies' failings, relational ties remain directed through modernity's *symbolic code* that directs the content of mediation in the form of values, symbols, rules, and instrumental resources (Donati 2011: 72).[7] Unless modernity's *symbolic code* is transcended, we are left with an epistemic observation system whose knowledge infrastructure is conceptually insular. Knowable reality takes the observer's starting point in the form of a pre-existing symbolic content that does not distinguish between the human element and outcomes sought from relations. Therefore, policy initiatives are inherently closed, incapable of authentically devolving authority in a way that acknowledges and responds to relational distinctions as a possible referential moment of transformation. Whether gravitating towards one pole or seeking to triangulate between these poles, the functionalist mode of governance limits what is possible.

Lib/lab compromises reproduce the system-based approach to policy without altering its general framework but differ from it by seeking adaptable responses to what is represented as a fast-changing world. In the coming chapters, I aim to investigate a new relational mode of knowing that does not pre-define the direction of social relations. As stated in this chapter, the *lib/lab* approach is conceptually incapable of acknowledging the human element's autonomy as a referential object of knowledge. Thus, a re-think is necessary to understand knowledge to be generated from the reciprocity of epistemic relations — the *a priori* origins from which knowledge develops. Starting from the relation's internal features opens new horizons of sociability — with transformative social bonds — that *morphogenetically* transcends the received.

---

7   An example of this regulation and formalising of relations was previously noted in New Labour's reliance on governance technologies and an ethos of managerialism to measure outputs. Similarly, the Conservative Party's English devolution plans, a theme that gained prominence under David Cameron's leadership and subsequently continued, demonstrate a regulated mediation of relations. The contract-based approach to English devolution — as the state steers contractual obligations with local authorities — meant local decision-making is tied to central government funding that sets the direction of partnerships and the organisational setting to produce desired outcomes (Sandford 2019). The noted case of increased infrastructure investment in local vocational education is an example of funding tied to a broader context of business skills needs and economic productivity.

Concluding Remarks

The documentation of different *lib/lab* approaches in this chapter demonstrates the hegemony of system-based forms of governance that seek to compromise between valorising self-governance and the collective regulation of this self-governance to ensure individuals are adequately integrated into the system needs. While differing in focus, the common denominator between these approaches is the proposal to transcend inherited ideological templates to meet the needs of a changing global economic order. Each attempted to enable individuals to adapt their behaviour through work-based forms of welfare that reward initiative and responsibility in different ways.

New Labour represented an approach that sought to reach a compromise through an enabling role for the state to integrate individuals into a broader state-defined national project. Accordingly, there was a narrative of a changing world that brings novel economic needs. In response, new policy formulations were needed to remedy an existing skills gap to meet these needs. The environmental contingencies needed an enabling state — the lab side of governance — to produce relevant opportunities for individuals to claim their stake. As a result, investment in the social aimed to tackle moral anomie and connect individuals to strategic networks (bridging social capital). The intended outcome of this process was the enablement of self-governance — the lib side — through responsible citizens contributing to creating a more viable market economy. Consequently, the New Labour compromise between lib and lab poles of governance was intended to enable a virtuous cycle in which the state directs networks to produce institutional arrangements that integrate citizens into broader governance goals.

The 'Big Society' agenda represented continuity rather than rupture with New Labour's *lib/lab* approach. Rhetorically, welfare co-production themes took greater prominence due to a proposed normative breakdown. Again, new policy initiatives advanced beyond pre-existing templates, that is, reliance on collective formations between the individual and state. These formations are vital as they are a bulwark against inherited inter-generational dependency — with responsibility eroded by the welfare state — by enabling individuals to take self-responsibility. The rolling forward of the 'Big Society' was directly tied to a state-engineered environment of self-governance. In this process, the state would remake the social by opening public services to partnerships that enable welfare co-production. Policy nudges were envisaged to direct individual choices and extended to collective initiatives to transform the decision-making context. Here, as with New Labour, we saw the same objective of re-thinking the social to be more responsive to skills needed in the economy. Though agreed on goals, the 'Big Society' differed in focus from New Labour by emphasising a broader normative breakdown and the need for collective changes to create the right structures and environment for individuals and communities to help themselves.

Both the 'Great Meritocracy and 'levelling-up' agendas represent a return to New Labour's focus on skills-based solutions to supply-side weaknesses, and the role government can take to make the economy work for everyone. They promoted the provision of opportunities in work-based training to ensure prosperity and get people into work. In turn, in the spirit of meritocratic fairness, increased opportunity meant that personal initiative would be rewarded, and everyone could advance based on merit. The envisioned outcome is that individuals make the most of their initiative and gain skills to grow the economy. Relatedly, Boris Johnson's 'levelling-up' rhetoric emphasised the importance of a 'fair deal' that delivers an 'opportunity guarantee'. The lab's role, here, was to ensure that individuals can access the right training to connect citizens to better jobs in the context of a productive nation. Infrastructure investment — the goal to 'build back better' — is an attempt to train individuals and connect them to high-skilled jobs. Thus, as with other *lib/lab* approaches, the state has a role in which it is part of a virtuous cycle that endows individuals with the requirements of roles that are well integrated into greater system needs.

These different approaches to *lib/lab* governance demonstrate a shared vision in which the state provides the tools for provision beyond what is represented as the ideological template of top-down governance. Yet, in attempting to transcend previous ideological templates, a state-led mutual socialisation of relations remains. The state provides the direction of organisational relations — including leadership structures — and the outcomes that are expected from these relations. As a result, notwithstanding the claims of transcending previous ideological templates, we have the reproductive continuity of modernity's symbolic code that negates distinctions within relations rather than acknowledging these distinctions as referential objects of knowledge. Specifically, the human element's reality and transformative potential are first understood from pre-existing symbolic content that shapes the identity and future of relations.

Therefore, as will be articulated in the coming chapters, it becomes necessary to propose an alternative epistemic approach that acknowledges the human element in social relations. The human element is the referential starting point that directs the identity of relations and their organisational ties. Subjective and objective dimensions are, thus, emergent from generative mechanisms that are characterised by the reciprocal orientations between agent-subjects (Donati 2011). Acknowledging reciprocity as a *sui generis* reality entails starting from the internal features of sociability rather than seeking to regulate its outcomes. Hence, the received templates are open to transformation through new ways of knowing that shape new sociability parameters. These, in turn, better meet the needs of those in relationships.

2. Relational Realism as an Alternative General Sociological Approach

This chapter examines the foundational assumptions of a relational realist approach. The aim is to provide an alternative general approach to functionalism and its system-based framework. In direct contrast with the system-based regulation of relations, the relational approach starts from the contingency of social reality to explore the determinants that are emergent from its interactive dynamics. Three points are covered in this chapter, which justifies the necessity of a general framework that guides the logic of social policies and interventions:

1. The necessity of referential detachment as the basis of *judgemental rationality*: Without referential detachment, it is impossible to progressively explain and interpret pre-existing determinants of social reality, that is, its *generative mechanisms*.

2. The articulation of referential detachment in a relational realist general approach: In a relational realist general approach, the object of analysis is explained in and through social relations, that is, reciprocal exchanges of knowing.

3. The reciprocal relationship between observer and observed is embedded in a structure of wider networks: A structure of wider networks organises human-referenced patterns of sociability that seek to develop the human element's latent potentiality. The aim is to generate networked interventions — grounded in epistemic relations between the observer and observed — that exceed the already given towards the potentially transformational.

The Necessity of Referential Detachment

The relationship between the referential act and the referent is articulated in the next section through the epistemic quadrangle model (Donati 2011). Before expanding on this epistemic approach, it is necessary first to justify a realist *philosophical ontology* based on referential detachment that starts from the relationality of social reality. In providing this justification, two general approaches — both denying the necessity of a *philosophical ontology* — are evaluated:

- Mid-range realism views any claim to a *philosophical ontology* as internally incoherent due to its epistemically transitive starting point.

- The understanding that any distinction between the act of reference and referent is a form of philosophising sociology. Instead, the centrality of practice is posited in which all theories are viewed as tools for action.

Mid-Range Realism

Mid-range realist theories agree in their rejection of transcendental realism as a *philosophical ontology*. The distinction between the act of reference and referent is acknowledged, but the act itself is considered a fallible conceptual model constituted in the transitive domain (Cruickshank 2004; 2010). As ontological claims are socially embedded, they are presupposed by a fallible interpretation that cannot act as an underlabourer operating outside the conditions of its emergence. Due to this fallibility, there can be no master definition of what constitutes social reality. The realist *philosophical ontology* sets itself the task of transposing questions of being into questions of knowledge despite the latter providing the content on how reality is epistemically mediated:

> The problem though is that in defining the epistemic fallacy as the transposing of questions about being into questions about knowing, Bhaskar has defined the said fallacy so broadly that any reference to what we know of reality (which may well be knowledge claims with a high degree veracity) must commit this putative fallacy (Cruickshank 2004: 572).

Therefore, to start from a *philosophical ontology* is to start from a vantage point independent of scientific knowledge. Such a position first posits what must be the case for science to be possible (Cruickshank 2004: 573). In this scenario, we have an irresolvable antinomy in which a metaphysical claim denies the grounds of its emergence. As a result, it is not plausible to distinguish a *philosophical ontology* from the substantive one due to the impossibility of a God's eye view to extrapolate the essential features of reality (Cruickshank 2004: 568).

In the case of mid-range realism[1], Cruickshank argues, it is possible to commit to ontological claims that are not transcendental. Instead of metaphysical claims, ontological presuppositions are recognised as being situated within the transitive domain — they are developed and revised in critical dialogue with other theories, whose adequacy is derived from their efficacy:

> Rather, ontological presuppositions may be recognised as being situated within the transitive domain, and that the task of social scientists is to draw upon the most useful ontological definitions that currently prevail in the transitive domain (Cruickshank 2004: 582).

Thus, in the transitive domain, any theory is intrinsic to practice and mediates our interaction (acts of reference) in the natural and discursive worlds.

Cruickshank proposes that situated ontological presuppositions can be realised in Popper's justification of knowledge growth in problems located in theory. Cruickshank's approach is iterative insofar as previously solved problems in an antecedent theory become subject to criticism and replaced by an alternative view (Cruickshank 2010: 600). Adopting this alternative approach re-formulates the *epistemic fallacy* so that it is substantively constituted as a fallibilist epistemology. Accordingly, ontological claims are open to revision and never settled:

---

1 Realism can be described as mid-level when it repudiates intransitive ontological presuppositions and the feasibility of research pragmatics with little theoretical insight or rigour (the idea of theory as emergent *a posteriori* from data collected). However, while repudiating the monological immanent critique of a *philosophical ontology*, the idea of 'internal coherence' is acknowledged, that is, that some models are progressively efficacious in producing useful ontological definitions. This commitment situates Cruickshank's approach as a midpoint between philosophical starting points and the primacy of research outcomes detached from theoretical considerations.

> This is a problem because if knowledge is held to be fallible then, rather than simply using this to say that one's claims are not infallible, one needs to put this recognition to work, so to speak. Doing this, one would argue that as knowledge claims are fallible, they need to be revised and replaced through criticism. This would be antithetical to the search for an answer to a transcendental question because one would not be seeking some fixed answer but rather holding that all forms of knowledge claim were open to revision and replacement (Cruickshank 2010: 598).

Kaidesoja argues similarly that transcendental arguments aim to postulate the 'general categorical structure of the world' (2013: 18). Specifically, conceptually, it is internally incompatible to appropriate Kantian transcendental arguments in a realist sense. Kant's view does not start from metaphysical speculations about the world's general categorical structure; instead, the starting point is the general categories of understanding of the epistemic subject (Kaidesoja 2013: 84). The Kantian synthetic *a priori* is a transcendental idealism that brings together, simultaneously, the structures of our understanding with the object of our experience (Kaidesoja 2013: 85). It is a view that does not justify *a priori* transcendental arguments from what is knowable *a posteriori*. In contrast to a Kantian synthetic *a priori*, transcendental realism aims to demonstrate the necessary conditions for the possibility of intelligible scientific practices (Kaidesoja 2013: 87).

Therefore, transcendental realism reverses the Kantian synthetic *a priori* when starting from what is posited as the world's general categorical structure. Due to this object-sided starting point (the question of being), it cannot convey a synthetic *a priori* that articulates the subjective conditions of knowing. The truth-value of scientific practice descriptions become presuppositions that dictate real people's activities in the real world (Kaidesoja 2013: 88 - 89). Without recourse to these activities, it is impossible to justify understandings pre-defined in the name of a *philosophical ontology*. Hence, it is irreconcilable to develop arguments *a posteriori* that, after that become transcendental necessities:

> It is not possible to justify a posteriori any propositions about transcendental necessities in the Kantian sense, because knowledge a posteriori is always merely hypothetical and hence fallible (Kaidesoja 2013: 90).

The fallible nature of realist transcendental arguments means they cannot dictate models and practices *a priori*. As 'naturalised transcendental arguments' start from reasoning that sets itself apart from the practices it seeks to systemise, there is no recourse to the situated activities of people in the real world to adjudicate between competing theories:

> Practices that are referred to in the premises of these supposedly 'naturalised transcendental arguments' can (in principle) always be interpreted from the point of view of two or more incompatible ontological theories and there is no a priori way to decide which interpretation is true (Kaidesoja 2013: 98).

What is the basis of *judgemental rationality* and progressive practice? Again, it relates to practices that develop from the transitive domain (a *substantive ontology*):

> I would thus say that the intelligibility and rationality of the practice X relate to our conceptions and judgements concerning this practice rather than the features of the world that make it possible in the first place (Kaidesoja 2013: 87).

The intrinsic features of good basic science are identified in the explanatory power of models and theories (Kaidesoja 2013: 100). Standards are not pre-justified but emerge according to different disciplines in which new theoretical ideas and methodologies are developed (Kaidesoja 2013: 101). Based on this inter-disciplinary view of epistemically successful scientific practices, particular understandings of social reality can be discounted as incompatible with the best theories of other sciences:

> This requirement is needed, because the most epistemically successful scientific practices presuppose that different sciences study the same world and that the results produced in different disciplines should be complementary, not contradictory. I find this requirement especially important in the context of social ontology, since, for example, physically reductionist, idealist and individualist views of the nature of social reality are not compatible with the best theories about human cognition proposed in cognitive sciences [...]. This means that arguments in naturalised social ontology are not solely based on the successful social scientific practices since their conclusions should also be compatible with the ontological assumptions of the empirically confirmed theories of other sciences (Kaidesoja 2013: 101).

Pragmatist Methodological Relationism

Kivinen & Piiroinen's (2006) pragmatist methodological relationism takes an altogether different position against referentialist ontological reasoning. This approach rejects any commitment to a 'metaphysical language game of ontology and what might be called a "referentialist" conception of knowledge' (Kivinen & Piiroinen 2006: 310). Here, any form of ontological reasoning is rejected, including the philosophical dualism of subject-object. What follows is the relationality of the object in which the object is never distinct from the knowing subject:

> Like Dewey ([1925] 1981, 173–225), we give up the whole philosophical subject-object dualism, which first presupposes the knowing subject as an entity distinct from the objects of its knowledge, and then engages in figuring out how the subject could form correct representations of the world (Kivinen & Piiroinen 2006: 309).

Fruitful methodological debates (sociologising philosophy) — in contrast to what are termed metaphysical theories — are concerned with people's concrete problems in their everyday social lives (Kivinen & Piiroinen 2006: 319). The knowing entity is already practically engaged and formed by shared practices. As engagement with the world is not independent of the referent — an object already named — it is the practical relations of their naming that becomes the object of inquiry:

> It is precisely because of the centrality of practice — because of the fact that everything is practical and can only be weighed in action — that all theories should be conceived of as nothing but tools for action (Kivinen & Piiroinen 2006: 319).

Following the Deweyan operationalist approach, a practical and problem-driven way of understanding the social sciences is reached. In this approach, all human knowledge is related to the inquirer's purposes, and all beliefs are to be weighed in intentional action and its consequences. The inquirer's social scientific conceptualisations are tools that must be rendered operational in things to be done. A sense of the rules of the game in the form of problems people face in their everyday lives is not something to be theorised to capture the complexity and contingency of the real world. Instead, what is advocated is a theory with a small 't' that is oriented towards solving research problems:

> From a pragmatist standpoint, we need to embrace the strict demand of operationalizability — understanding theories in terms of acts to be done — and this means, among other things, dropping the idea that the growing complexity of a theory and the use of peculiar doctrinal lexicon can be justified by the claim that they are needed in capturing the complexity and indefiniteness of the real world (cf. Bourdieu and Wacquant 1992, 22—23, and n. 40 and 41). Rather, we need an unambiguously operationalisable frame of references (i.e., a simple theory with a small t) that serves us as a practicable toolset for solving specific research problems (Kivinen & Piiroinen 2006: 319–320).

The Inconsistencies of Theories that Oppose Transcendental Reasoning

Both theories, mid-range realism and pragmatist methodological relationism, represent two different critiques of transcendental reasoning. The objections of both these views will next be reviewed, and two responses will be presented to justify the necessity of a *philosophical ontology*. The necessity of a *philosophical ontology* follows from the internal inconsistencies of mid-range realism and pragmatist methodological relationism:

1. The idea of a distinction between the act of reference and object of reference — an idea acknowledged by mid-range realism — requires a general analytical approach to examine the relationship between both.

2. The pragmatist methodological relationism described above denies the need for any general approach despite relying on a *philosophical ontology*.

In response to mid-range realism, the possibility of *judgemental rationality* is presupposed by the distinction between the observer and the observed, whose terms of reference are meaningful in the mediation within the relation of reference. As Tyfield (2007) argues, it is the ontological properties of the relatum ('our ontology') that determines the relation of reference:

> As with all relations, the nature of the relatum of the permissible objects of reference, i.e., our ontology, necessarily determines the nature of the relation of reference (Tyfield 2007: 151).

We are dealing with a reciprocal exchange — a dialogue — between the act of reference and the referent. The *a priori* framework of transcendental realism does not impose a fixed answer on the parameters of knowing. Instead, it affirms knowing to be emergent from the contingency of social reality, whose first ontological premise is the relation itself (Donati 2011). Social reality is understood and interpreted from the perspective of the relation that provides context and makes the observed an intelligible object of investigation (the object being both pre-existing but also contingently emergent from its relations of reference). Thus, the relationality of social reality requires an analytical paradigm that can investigate the interconnections between the relation's elements that generate its differentiated features, i.e., its properties and powers.

When investigating the interconnections of the relation — between observer and observed — we are called to detach the referential act from that which it refers. As Bhaskar argues, it is this necessary procedure of detachment that establishes distinctiveness in the relation that is articulated from the viewpoint of the referent (the intransitive dimension):

> The procedure which I have called 'referential detachment', that is, the detachment of the act of reference from that to which it refers, establishes at once the existential separation, distinctiveness or 'intransitivity' of both referential act and referent and the possibility of another reference to either, a condition of any intelligible discourse at all (Bhaskar 2000: 24).

The existential separation means that while the observer and observed are embedded in their context, the pre-existence of the observed implicates an 'intransitivity' between the referential act and referent. Simultaneously, the contingent mediation — a relation of knowing — between the referential act and referent is the access point and necessary condition of intelligible discourse. Thus, the process of referential detachment means a separation at the moment of reference — it is not an attitude that 'epistemalogizes or normalises ontology' (Bhaskar 2007: 194). Instead, it opens the door to epistemic relativity and the practice of *judgmental rationality* towards the referent's 'intransitivity'. We have a *philosophical ontology* that is intrinsically deduced from epistemic relations between the observer and observed, making judgment possible. The transcendental reasoning of relational realism is not a starting point that takes, for example, a functionalist system perspective that externally pre-establishes the parameters of knowing.

As the epistemic relation between the referential act and referent is internal to the relation and contingent, we are led to an *a posteriori* explanation derived from the dynamics of environmental interaction. Sociological knowledge derived from social reality — a reality that possesses relational properties and powers from its interactive dynamics — translates into relational concepts and observations. Therefore, there is a simultaneity between sociological knowledge and social reality — just as social reality possesses relational properties and powers, the same applies to sociological knowledge (Donati 2011: 103).

As sociological knowledge, like social reality, is a relational product of social agency, the observer's agency is interwoven with the agency of the observed. Between both is the mediation of pre-existing structural and cultural forms that generate the properties and powers of both social reality and sociological knowledge. The relation between social reality and sociological knowledge implicates an analytical perspective that derives its legitimacy from within the space-time of the social relation. The result of the process of mediated interaction is the development of new structural, cultural, and agential forms (Donati 2011: 99).

Sociological knowledge, therefore, derived from social reality, is inseparable from referential detachment that starts from the dynamics of the epistemic relationship. The question is whether or not the starting point acknowledges the referent's perspective and the range of relations that underlie its formation. Again, as the internal dynamics of the relation is the first ontological starting point, there are no fixed answers that normalise ontology through a pre-given referential perspective (as is the case in system-based governance discussed in the previous chapter).

On the other hand, pragmatist methodological relationism replaces referential detachment with unceasing cycles of practice-based problem-solving within self-referential networks. Two central problems can be identified with this general approach:

1. Despite its claim that it rejects 'philosophical sociology', albeit, through negation, it adopts a general approach, that is, theory with a capital 'T'.

2. Denying the necessity of referential detachment leaves us with no way to evaluate the efficacy of practices.

Regarding the first point, self-referential relations of knowing — with no distinction accepted between the referential act and referent — is an *a priori* framework whose defining factor is an already named world weighed in action. Consequently, there is a closed transcendental *philosophical ontology* that denies its starting point through negation. The present tense focus on action-centred relations means the immanence of communicative networks encapsulates all differences, including the distinction between the knower and the world. From to this starting point, all theory is merely a language game within networks of self-referential practice.

The negation of the difference between the referential act and referent means there is a pre-given conceptual evaluation with no distinction between a linguistic knowing-that and embodied knowing-how. As a result, as analytical ties disappear between the propositional and embodied experience, we are left with empiricism at the level of events. Answering research questions and solving problems, in this general approach, leads to an empiricist mode of observation that focuses on immediate interactive communication on who is doing what and when, i.e., on how individuals manage social mechanisms at the level of events. Implicated from this a priori framework, due to its presentism and analytical conflation, is both the genetic and *epistemic fallacy*.

Second, the interpretive paradigm that follows from pragmatist methodological relationism is conceptually incapable of evaluating the efficacy of methods it uses when seeking answers to research questions. The pragmatic relational general approach, committing the *epistemic fallacy*, disconnects the linguistic knowing-that — the referential act — from the embodied knowing-how. Absent from this account are the contingent, relational dynamics that generate observed determinants. As we are conceptually operating at the level of meanings, we are disconnected from the underlying reality that produces new relationships that explain the origins of properties and powers of referents investigated. In self-referential operative practices, we only have self-referential networks of meanings. Consequently, research cannot be anchored in anything distinguished from de-centred practices weighed in action.

An Epistemic Framework in which a Compass is the Referent's Relations of Emergence

As the epistemic relation — the necessary condition of intelligible discourse — is the first ontological premise of social reality, a general framework is needed to articulate the interchange between the referential act and referent. We are not merely focused on what individuals do to manage social mechanisms in their immediate activities. Instead, the focus is on relational networks that are operationalised through a process of *double contingency*. Based on the *double contingency* between *Ego and Alter*, existential separation and 'intransitivity' operate at all levels of society that make up the environment of emergence. A relational realist general approach aims to analytically explore the contingency in this environment that impacts the referent's *latent ontological reality* as a *generative mechanism*.

Generative mechanisms are more than exercised powers immediately perceived in events (Prandini 2011: 41). As a transcendent reality irreducible to its context, the object's latent model points to its mode of operation — the potential properties it could develop in alternative relational settings. The distinction and interrelation between the latent mode of operation — the transcendent mode of existence — and the environment that mediates its development is the basis of referential detachment. Based on this distinction, the epistemic model consists of two triangles that, when placed one above the other, form a quadrangle (Donati 2011, see Figure 1):

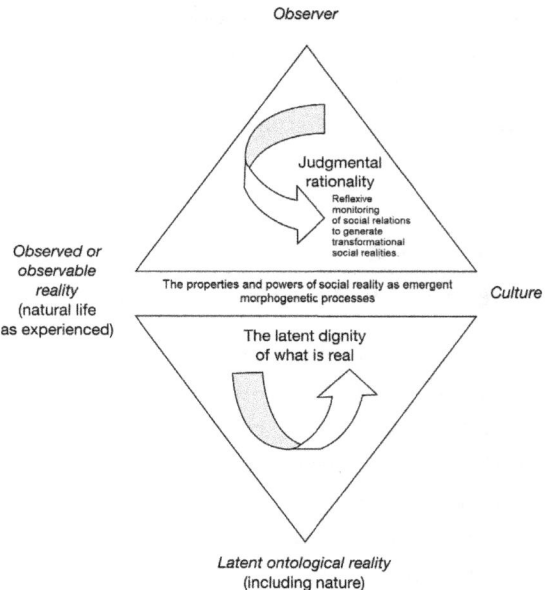

Fig. 1 For relational sociology, critical realism is an approach that extends the epistemic triangle (commonly used in sociology: observer — culture — observed reality — latent ontological reality) (Donati 2011: 100). The diagram is adapted to show the epistemic quadrangle in the context of social interventions generating transformational social realities.

1. The first (upper) triangle refers to the observer whose immediate scope of perception is the object's observable reality (the level of the event).

2. The second (lower) triangle of the quadrangle refers to the *latent ontological reality* of the perceived object.

The distance between the upper and lower triangle denotes existing relational mediations (referential acts). In the relation between both triangles, the act of reference conveys *judgemental rationality* towards the second triangle, that is, the underlying reality that generates exercised powers. In the interrelation between observer and observed, *judgemental rationality* (as a reflexive mediation) expresses the potentially transformational in the context of patterns of sociability intended to enable the development of the referent as a *Relational Subject*. Hence the dialogical relation between the upper and lower triangles implicates the reflexive monitoring of existing relations in their efficacy in generating transformational social realities.

The epistemic quadrangle proposes a general approach to understanding social reality as complex networks managed in reciprocal and contingent relations (the epistemic process of *double contingency*). It is an epistemic framework that establishes a general understanding from which we evaluate (using *judgemental rationality*) the properties and powers of social reality as mediations emergent from the interplay of its constituent elements, that is, the dynamic between actors and broader socio-cultural properties and powers. The *morphogenetic paradigm* is derived from this relational realist understanding as an analytical logic and language to investigate the internal dynamics of relations and outcomes produced through these dynamics.[2] In turn, the methodological tools devised when answering a research question aim to empirically validate the interactions of pre-existing determinants to ascertain the outcomes they produce.

The process described above are components of sociology as a knowledge system and apply to any general theory that seeks to understand and solve problems relating to research questions (Donati 2011: 105). Whether implicit or explicit, affirming or denying, any attempt to answer questions, as argued before, starts from a general approach that impacts the explanatory paradigm and methodological tools adopted. If social reality is understood as the reality of 'social facts' that are emergent relational products, then the paradigm, tools, and theories developed should express this understanding. Thus, utilising the AGIL scheme as a compass, Donati (2011) posits four cardinal points of sociology as a knowledge system (see Figure 2):

1. A general approach or metatheory (L) that affirms an understanding of social reality. This general approach can be stated as a *philosophical ontology*.

2. Derived from a general approach is a compatible paradigm (I) whose premises express and apply the metatheory. As the relational realist framework starts from the relations that generate observed reality, we need an analytical paradigm to explore the complexity

---

2 In the case of a relational realist approach, the *morphogenetic paradigm* is a complementary paradigm that can analyse the interchanges within relations over time. The paradigm will be covered in more detail in Chapter Three.

of analytical exchanges that constitute this reality. In relational realism, the *morphogenetic paradigm* explains outcomes as dynamic relations between agency and evolving structures.

1. Methodological research tools (A) operationalise morphogenetic processes. Specifically, they identify appropriate tools that answer questions based on an analytical understanding of social reality as networks of reciprocal interchanges.
2. Single theories (G) are derived from research outcomes that reflect a relational realist understanding of social reality.

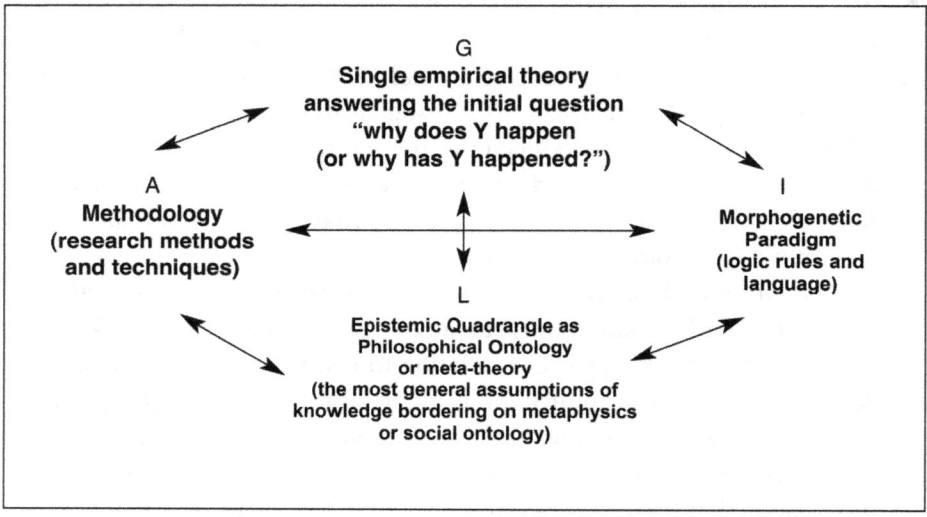

Fig. 2 The components of sociology as a knowledge system (aimed at formulating a theory) built upon two axes, L-G and A-I (Donati 2011: 105). The diagram is adapted to relational realism and the *morphogenetic paradigm*.

Based on the four sociological knowledge points, we start from the reasoned necessity of an *a priori* starting point. Based on this starting point, an analytical language is derived that applies *judgemental rationality* to the referent's conditions of emergence. In turn, to study the conditions of emergence, equally relational tools are needed to answer research questions and develop theories.

Networked Interventions that Surpass the already Given towards the Potentially Transformational

Adoption of the general approach, based on how social relations are understood, produces implications for the direction of social interventions. In the epistemic quadrangle, observation involves explaining the object in reference to its underlying *latent ontological reality*. Based on the interaction of agent-subjects, the relational mediations between both triangles provide the context for the emergence of the lower triangle. Referential detachment is applied in the mediations of agents-subjects through *judgemental rationality*, which normalises ontology. The relational *symbolic code* is operationalised in these morphogenetic interactions to arrive at *judgemental rationality* in networked interconnections between personal and social outcomes.

In these interwoven relations, network analysis explores the differentiation and mutual interaction between the human and social. It acknowledges the networked reality between the non-contingency of pre-existing human needs and the social order whose patterns of sociability meet these needs. Modernity's *symbolic code* and its functionalist *modus operandi* cannot distinguish between these distinctions of relations because its starting point is the system and the needs of the social order (Donati 2011: 162).

Derived from a relational model of reference, the relationship between the immanent (*judgemental rationality*) and transcendent (the latent dignity of what is real) dimensions of social reality implicate networked interventions that can articulate the distinction between the human and social. This networked logic is the practical application of a social ontology whose starting premise is the reciprocal interchange between *Ego and Alter* — whether individual or collective actors (these interchanges exist in relations between the upper and lower triangles of the epistemic triangle). Recursively, the reality generated in the lower triangle is emergent from and embedded in complex networks that make up the mediation between the two triangles. Again, as network analysis explores the relations between these mediations, the application of *judgemental rationality* becomes key. It is the normative dimension that is identified and emergent from the mediation between the upper and lower triangles.

Policy initiatives and interventions are an outcome of network analysis between the upper and lower triangles; they develop from the relation's epistemic interchanges to determine sought outcomes. As will be expanded in the coming chapters, the *morphogenetic paradigm* is a model that explores the inner dynamics of these epistemic relations by analysing their reflexive interplay that produces structural bonds. The paradigm is equipped to explore the referential acts of its participants that normatively regulate the relation between the human and social. As a result, the aim of *morphogenetic cycles* is to ensure interventions continuously direct potentially transformative interventions in the mediations between the upper and lower triangles in the spirit of *judgemental rationality*.

Concluding Remarks

This chapter proposed an alternative approach to system-based functionalism, the ethos of which dominates policy models and initiatives. In contrast to the external regulation of relations, the relational realist approach starts from the contingency of social reality to explore how it mediates the emergence of relational elements — both actors and the social order. The idea of a general approach that underpins an alternative policy vision was justified as a reasoned necessity.

Two opposing perspectives on the concept of *philosophical ontology* were presented. In contrast to mid-range realism, relational realism is not a metaphysical ontology that transposes questions of knowing into questions of being. Rather, its first ontological premise is grounded in epistemic relations from which the relatum is emergent. Relational realism also contrasts methodological relationism, a metaphysical starting point that only acknowledges the doings of knowing subjects. With no distinction between the doings of the knowing subject and engagement with the referent, there is no way to evaluate the efficacy of practices. Hence, methodological relationism is a closed metaphysical ontology that denies its ontological presupposition despite starting from the purposes of inquiry rather than outcomes irreducible to the practical understandings of social scientific practice.

With a *philosophical ontology* being a reasoned necessity, a model to operationalise epistemic relations is needed. If efficacious referential acts are continuously regenerated, then an epistemic model should connect the process of referential detachment to transformative mediations. The epistemic quadrangle understands these mediations to be embedded in networked connections in which reciprocal interchanges exist at both the level of the event and the broader socio-cultural context that shapes the direction of these interchanges. Progressive problem-solving, therefore, mediates between the upper and lower triangles. These mediations acknowledge the referent's developmental emergence as an irreducible and emergent *generative mechanism* (the *latent ontological reality* of the referent). In the process of referential detachment, existing mediations in the interplay between immanence and transcendence generate the properties and powers of social reality.

Social policy initiatives attuned to the referent (Alter) require the reflexive monitoring of existing mediations in their capacity to generate transformative patterns of sociability. Accordingly, based on the relational realist general approach, an analytical paradigm is needed to investigate the interplay within relations and the outcomes they produce. The *morphogenetic paradigm*, discussed in the following chapters, approaches the different elements of social reality — both the personal and the socio-cultural — as networked phenomena. It is a paradigm that views epistemic mediations from within the relation (a networking logic) to develop *meta-reflexive* subjects that actively participate in the regeneration of the social order rather than relying on a compromise between impersonal system mechanisms and individualised preferences. Therefore, the contingency of current mediations is not the point of reproductive adaptation but the basis of reflection on how things could be different. Again, relational realism opposes closed ontologies that limit the possible by regulating the parameters of sociability.

3. The Morphogenetic Paradigm: Conceptualising the Human in the Social

In this chapter, I aim to explore the implications of the relational realist approach to the question of personhood. The *morphogenetic paradigm*, derived from relational realism, approaches this question through the relational and stratified interplay between social- and personal-identity properties. This interdependence accounts for the emergence of personal identity and is fundamental to how referential acts valorise the human element in policies and practices. If we are to valorise the human in the social — as will be discussed in the coming chapters — then it is necessary to explain the relational co-emergence of both. Thus, to enter the dynamics of relations is to identify how social processes mediate the emergence of personal identity.

Inside the relation, we identify the perspective of persons through the properties and powers of 'internal deliberations'. Starting from the developmental input point of persons, policies and practices are referential acts that become better attuned to the *latent reality* of the human-in-the-social. Interventions that are developed in conjunction with subjective input, it will be argued, consider the interactive dynamics between personal, collective, and social reflexivity that anchor the process of social morphogenesis. The emphasis on the interactive dynamics of the relations will be investigated in terms of a social ecology that synergistically produces primary and secondary *relational goods*. *Relational goods* are vital to sustaining a morphogenetic social order whose parameters are continuously expanded in a transcendental way.

The Interdependence between the Properties of Social Relations and the Emergence of Personal Identity

In the *morphogenetic paradigm*, an internal conversation links the human and the social. An efficacious internal conversation is presupposed by the self's irreducible subjective authority concerning its wider environment. To investigate personal morphogenesis is to trace its trajectory from the initial sense of self — embodied and emergent from the natural and practical orders — to the development of personal identity. In the coming sections, I will argue that the initial sense of self provides the vantage point from which subjective interiority and authority are made possible. The development of personal identity that arises from the self's unique vantage point gives the process of personal morphogenesis its irreducible, subjective properties. Any relation that operates relationally, that is, that deals with the problem of social integration in reference to those in relation, should strategise its initiatives from the perspective and trajectory of personal development.

The developmental trajectory of personal identity is a relational property in which internal deliberations are the link between mind and world. These deliberations are characterised by being world-directed and Personal Emergent Properties (PEP). Based on the interplay between personal deliberations and the world, Archer (2003) distinguishes socio-cultural structures ('context') from the deliberations and contribution of active agents ('concerns') (Archer 2003: 348). The interiority of internal deliberations has the potential to transform the world that cannot be rendered as something impersonal; in other words, internal deliberations are irreducible to the objectivity of third-person ideas:

> Because the properties and powers of 'internal deliberations' pertain to people, they cannot be expropriated from them and rendered as something impersonal. This would be to destroy their status as a personal emergent property (PEP). Thus the 'interiority' of the internal conversation cannot be exteriorised as 'behaviour', which could be impersonally understood by all. Similarly, the 'subjectivity' of inner dialogue cannot be transmuted into 'objectivity', as if first-person thoughts could be replaced by third-person ideas. Finally, the personal causal efficacy of our deliberation

cannot be taken over the forces of 'socialisation': this would be to replace the power of the person for the power of society (Archer 2003: 94).

Thus, without irreducible interiority, there can be no subjective authority over the forces of socialisation. The properties of subjective interiority generate powers that are relational properties operating between mind and world:

> The internal conversation is a personal emergent property (a PEP) rather than a psychological 'faculty' of people, meaning some intrinsic human disposition. This is because inner conversations are relational properties, and the relations in question are those which obtain between mind and world (Archer 2003: 94).

The relations between mind and world, the prerequisite of transformative action, is the foundational question of how people distance themselves from their biological origins in a process of social becoming (that is, a trajectory of ongoing development). According to Archer, there are human properties and powers in this middle ground between the two, that is, an irreducible 'self-consciousness, reflexivity and a goodly knowledge of the world, which is indispensable to thriving in it' (Archer 2000: 189). The preparation for social becoming affirms an irreducible capability of hermeneutics from a first-person perspective. The importance of this reflexive middle ground is to maintain a clear subjective-objective distinction that upholds an irreducible capability of hermeneutics from a first-person perspective. This first-person perspective, with its irreducible subjective authority and interiority, is logically and ontologically before any social role. To compromise the subject-object distinction is to affirm the human merely as a bundle of molecules engaged in social interactions:

> Indeed, it has been argued here that a human being who is capable of hermeneutics has first to learn a good deal about himself or herself, about the world, and about the relations between them, all of which is accomplished through praxis. In short, the human being is both logically and ontologically prior to the social being, whose subsequent properties and powers need to build upon human ones. There is therefore no direct interface between molecules and meanings, for between them stretches this hugely important middle ground of practical life in which our emerging properties and powers distance us from our biological origins and prepare us for our social becoming (Archer 2009: 90).

As inner conversations are relational properties, three residual problems figure in the relation between mind and world. These three problems pertain to the temporal phases of active deliberations (internal dialogues) in which the self adapts its personal identity:

1. The generic problem of 'how can the self be both subject and object at the same time?' (Archer 2003: 94).

2. The analytical problem of who is speaking to whom when considering the temporal question of personal emergence, that is, the inner dialogue and the personal morphogenesis between past, present, and future selves.

3. The explanatory problem pertains to how the societal gets into the internal conversation. It explores the necessity of PEP and how the societal, as an order, is then mediated by these powers.

First, I will explore the foundational question of irreducible interiority as a prerequisite for transformative subjective powers. Afterwards, I will examine the implications of the fundamental question of how the three residual problems noted above are conceptualised. I will argue that the idea of reflexivity does not prepare us for our social becoming. Instead, the trajectory of personal morphogenesis in developmental terms — the unique way the indexical 'I' is individually sensed as a socially indexed device (Archer 2003: 91) — is what gives internal deliberations their irreducible transformative powers.

The Powers of Internal Deliberation: The Middle Ground between Meanings and Molecules

Subjective moments are expressed through the properties of internal deliberation. The morphogenetic process that explains the emergence of the personal identity starts from the subjective interiority of a fundamental sense of self. The properties and powers of this fundamental sense of self enable the authority of the personal identity as it dedicates itself to a social role. Although this process of deliberation is directed towards the world, it references a constellation of concerns that are emergent from the natural, practical, and discursive orders.[1] These orders generate

---

[1] Each of these orders generates distinct concerns that need to be navigated and reflexively configured by an emergent personal identity. According to Archer, 'A

conflicts that require navigation via inner dialogue to establish personal prioritisation and a preference schedule of ultimate concerns. When persons prioritise some concerns over others, a *modus vivendi*, they arrive at a behavioural outcome when dedicating themselves to a particular path. Archer (2009) develops the *DDD scheme* to conceptualise this process of prioritisation as a transition from *discernment* to *deliberation* to, finally, *dedication*.

The first-person phenomenon of reflexivity is the starting point in this process and is cognitive rather than merely perceptual (Archer 2003). Persons, that is, must be self-conscious and reflexive selves in order to be capable of hermeneutics. Based on this stratified view, persons are emergent from selves, and the social self is a subset of a broader personal identity that is forged in the DDD process (Archer 2000; 2009). The *morphogenetic paradigm* acknowledges the trajectory of the personal identity, describing the development of the indexical 'I' from being individually sensed to becoming a socially indexed device (Archer 2003: 91). This indexical 'I' — the fundamental sense of self — conceives itself independently of a name or other third-person referential device. Subjective interiority, in the self-attribution of mental states, affirms subjective authority over the process and outcomes of reflexive deliberation:

> I can conceive of myself quite independently of a name, a description or any other third-person referential device; reflexivity is quintessentially a first-person phenomenon (Archer 2003: 40).

A self-referenced internal conversation — the link between mind and world — is thus a conceptual necessity if internal deliberations are to be efficacious. Unless there is self-knowledge of beliefs, desires, intentions, and memories, then there can be no way to explain how an individual dedicates him or herself to specific role requirements and the manner through which this decision is reached:

> Unless people accepted that obligations were incumbent upon them themselves, unless they accepted role requirements as their own,

---

distinct type of concern derives from each of these orders. The concerns at stake are respectively those of "physical well-being" in relation to the natural order, "performative competence" in relation to the practical order, and "self-worth" in relation to the social order' (Archer 2011: 88).

or unless they owned their preferences and consistently pursued a preferences schedule, then nothing would get done in society (Archer 2003: 30).

Subjective deliberation in pursuit of a preference schedule is grounded in the interiority of a fundamental sense of self. This interiority presupposes subjective authority in its dedication to social roles. Before being made public, to confirm irreducibility to the discursive world, internal deliberations must be private. These originate with the transcendental indexical 'I'. What makes possible the efficacy of the 'I' as a subjective authority is reflexivity itself. Reflexive deliberation, a mental activity performed in private, leads to behavioural outcomes about what decisions to take and how to act. The irreducibility of this first-person perspective is thus the 'transcendentally necessary condition' (Archer 2003: 31) through which it is possible for the individual sense of self to self-referentially deliberate and dedicate (that is, to commit externally):

> reflexivity itself ... [is] a second-order activity in which the subject deliberates upon how some item, such as a belief, desire, idea or state of affairs pertains or relates to itself. By definition, reflexivity's first port of call has to be the first-person and the deliberation, however short, must be private before it can have the possibility of going public ... Hence 'reflexive deliberation' is the mental activity which, in private, leads to self-knowledge: about what to do, what to think and what to say (Archer 2003: 26).

The properties of internal deliberation establish the centrality of reflexivity in our social becoming. As we shall see later, this also anchors the process of social morphogenesis in persons due to internal deliberations being the link between the mind and the world. In an emphasis on the trajectory of personal identity, with primacy ascribed to embodied practical relations, the objective is to guard against sociological imperialism that emphasises public involvement (Archer 2003: 106).

Primacy is ascribed to the practical relations between meanings (discursive world) and molecules (biological capacities), and it is our reflexive capacity in practical relations that prepares us for our social becoming. Archer's presupposition is that this position of primacy is necessary to avoid the appropriation of subjective interiority, authority, and efficacy to public involvement.

The Three Residual Problems of the Internal Conversation

In asserting the first-person dimension of reflexivity, Archer implicates three residual problems of the internal conversation, as noted above. These start from the human capacity to be reflexive, which is the foundation of emergent personal identity — the consequences of this developmental progression anchor the processes of double and triple morphogenesis. I will suggest revisions to Archer's position following a detailed overview of the three problems. The revisions propose that reflexivity, in a developmental sense, is a third-person phenomenon that is actualised according to the unique trajectory of its emergence.

The first residual problem — the generic problem — relates to subjective interiority as a property of internal deliberation. It refers to self-awareness that bends backwards, that is, the alternation of the 'I' between states as subject and object. In this interplay, the world-directed experience becomes an object of self-conscious subjective manipulation. Therefore, the relational practical 'know-how' that generates these experiences is emergent from an initial being-in-the-world. The subjective manipulation of world-directed experiences bolsters the distinction between self and otherness:

> I can self-consciously manipulate the dialectic relationship between self and otherness and, in this very process, I reinforce the distinction between the two (Archer 2000: 130).

Asserting a subjective moment in the dialectic relationship between self and other yields a universal sense of self that necessarily precedes the emergence of the social self. Consequently, there must be efficacy in subjective moments to initiate the internal deliberative process that, after that, dedicates itself externally. Such world-directed deliberation generates a constellation of emergent concerns from the discursive, natural, and practical orders. One must navigate these often-conflicting concerns:

> These are concerns about our physical well-being in the natural order, about our performative achievement in the practical order and about our self-worth in the social order (Archer 2003: 120).

Relations to the natural order establish the first point of the self/otherness distinction by grounding the subjective 'know-how' emergent from the practical order with its constraints and enablements. The practical order acts as a bridge that secures meaning from embodied engagement in the natural order. Therefore, the irreducibility of the subjective response to societal meanings comes from deliberation about the properties of three ontologically distinct orders. As covered in the previous section, before taking on the social order, the individual human being is both logically and ontologically prior to the social being; social properties and powers are necessarily built upon pre-existing human ones (Archer 2000: 190). Between molecules and meaning is a pivotal role ascribed to the practical order: it is a middle ground that helps to 'distance us from our biological origins and prepare us for our social becoming' (Archer 2000: 190). Important human properties and powers emerge in the practical order — namely, a reflexive capacity and knowledge of the world:

> There is much more to the human being than a biological bundle of molecules plus society's conversational meanings. In fact, between the two, and reducible to neither, emerge our most crucial human properties and powers — self-consciousness, reflexivity, and a goodly knowledge of the world, which is indispensable to thriving in it (Archer 2000: 189).

The practical order's pivotal role does not disappear with the emergence of the propositional. Instead, the practical order continuously sustains society's conversational meanings via human properties and powers. The sense of self, emergent from embodied practical engagement, is a necessary precursor that sustains an emergent self-concept capable of transforming society's conversational meanings. Continuity of the sense of self is substantiated by the presence of procedural and eidetic memory that remains beyond the development of self-concept and whose recall is non-discursive. The non-linguistic recall relates directly to a sense of self engaged in its environment — it is through this engagement that there is a self/otherness distinction and a referential detachment inseparable from an understanding of space, time, and causality that are derived from sense data. The continuity of consciousness in both eidetic and procedural memory recalls the sedimentation of accomplished practical acts that form the basis of the 'habitual body' and self-identity. The habitual body conveys a past-tense practical accomplishment that enables human beings to contemplate the future. Declarative memory and self-knowledge are developmentally dependent and emergent from this prior constitution. Importantly, any declarative memory-activity never replaces the central role of the non-linguistic component:

> memory, far from being some intellectualised representation, is the bodily sedimentation of accomplished acts: it is the 'habitual body' which gives our past tense and enables us to contemplate a future, even though our embodied expectations have continuously to be reconciled with the dynamic nature of our existence in the world (Archer 2000: 132).

As the capability of hermeneutics is built on the capacities and powers of the human being, propositional knowledge does not exclusively constitute the direction of the semantic capability. The interplay between subject and object takes into account the properties and powers of objects approached as embodied, practical, and discursive knowledge. All three forms of knowledge shape the situations and circumstances that the subject then deliberates upon as part of their personal projects:

> All knowledge entails an interplay between properties and powers of the subject and properties and powers of the object — be this what we can learn to do in nature (embodied knowledge), the skills we can acquire in practice (practical knowledge), or the propositional elaborations we can make in the Cultural System (discursive knowledge). Any form of knowledge thus results from a confluence between our human powers (PEPs) and the powers of reality — natural, practical and social. Thus what have been discussed sequentially are the physical powers of the natural order, the material affordances and constraints of material culture, and, lastly, the logical constraining powers of the Cultural System. However, for the three orders equally, the way in which they affect the subject is by shaping the situations in which he or she find themselves, and their supplying constraints or enablements in relation to the subjects' projects (Archer 2000: 177).

The second residual problem of the internal conversation (the analytical problem) explores the efficacy of the subjective/objective interplay, considering the dialogue between past, present, and future selves. If the generic problem is concerned with the nature of relations between the subjective and objective from the perspective of world-directed internal deliberations — the basis of what Archer states as the self-conscious manipulation of the relation between self and otherness (Archer 2003: 130) — then the second residual problem deals with the enactment of Personal Emergent Properties (PEP) from the perspective of personal morphogenetic outcomes. The efficacy of the enactment of PEP is expressed in the materialisation of subjective alignment between social and personal identities. The analytical problem, associated with the emergence of the personal identity (subjective alignment), investigates how collective contexts interact with PEP to generate system outcomes, that is, the structure and distribution of positions that the Actor takes up.

As subjective alignment is the product of internal deliberations, the question is raised of how this alignment can be traced logically and temporally. The answer lies in PEP, which logically pre-supposes the Agent and the social position of the Actor. Human capacities (PEP) enable the individual's personification of roles based on reflexive adaptation to the properties and powers of collectives they face. These roles are classed as Primary Agency and Corporate Agency (Archer: 2000). Due to the logical primacy of PEP, the efficacy of internal deliberations is temporally charted to changes in both personal identity and society's normativity. It starts from the irreducible 'I' that encounters and deliberates on the properties of its natal context (Primary Agency (Me)). The natal context (Me) of the 'I' generates pre-dispositions and influences concerns relating to resources, life chances, etc. Nevertheless, the logical primacy of PEP means it is subjective deliberations that lead either to the reproduction or an attempt to transform the natal context (see quadrants one and two in Figure 3). As a result, the dedication to transform the natal context (Me) leads to the 'I' adopting the transformative role of Corporate Agency (We) that seeks to change both personal identity (You) and society's normativity (see quadrants three and four in Figure 3).

3. The Morphogenetic Paradigm: Conceptualising the Human in the Social

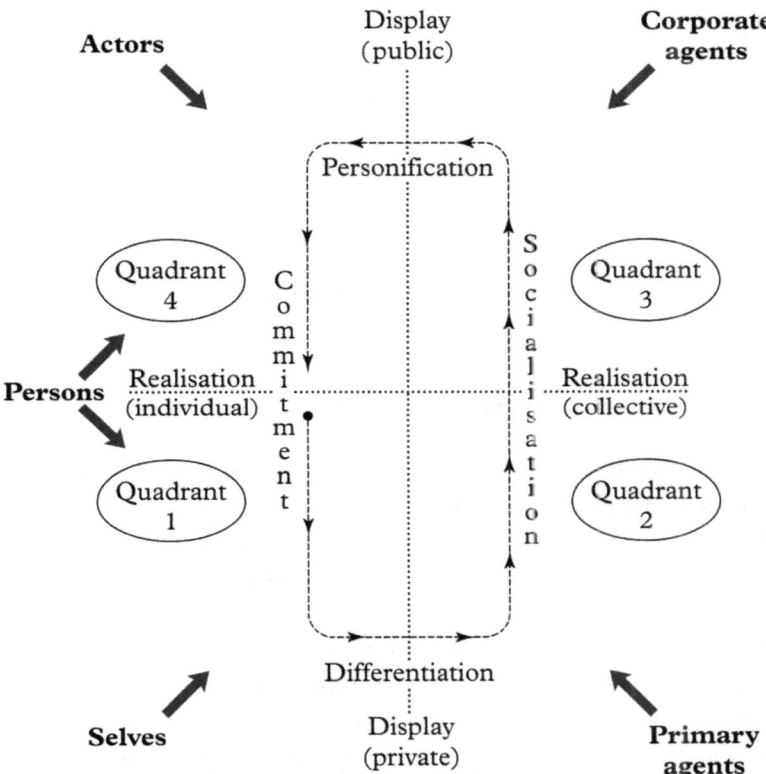

Fig. 3 Realism's account of the development of the stratified human being (Archer 2000: 260).

At the point of dedication, the personal identity (You) is subjectively aligned to its social identity (see Figure 4). The logical primacy of the 'I' — deliberating on unique concerns generated from its interaction with each relational order — renders social identity a subset of personal identity. Hence without self-identification with the role of Actor, through the properties and powers of Agency, it is not possible for society's normativity to either reproduce or transform itself. Therefore, the systemic outcomes produced are anchored in the reflexive capacities of persons — their internal conversations — as they become Agents. The explanation of system outcomes follows from the interrelated interaction between personal reflexivity and Agency.

the conditioned 'Me' – Primary Agent	
T1	T2

	the interactive 'We' – Corporate Agent
	T3

	the elaborated 'You' – PI + SI
	T4

Fig. 4 The emergence of personal and social identity (Archer 2000: 296).

Consequently, the third residual problem — the explanatory problem — looks at the outcomes of interactive dynamics (the second residual problem) in the emergence of social positions and their underlying structures. It aims to explain outcomes vis-à-vis the process of personal morphogenesis and its impact on Agency and Actor. To reiterate, when the 'I' is dissatisfied with its initial position — the 'Me' — it leads to a commitment to transform the original natal context and, subsequently, society's normativity. Hence, the co-emergence of the human, Agent, and Actor is examined as part of relational morphogenetic processes that mutually affect each other.

The morphogenesis of Agency is pre-supposed by personal morphogenesis in the personal identity ascribing to itself a social position. In turn, this dedication entails reproductive or transformative social actions that initiate structural or cultural morphostasis/morphogenesis, that is, the reproduction or transformation of the socio-cultural context. In the case of social morphogenesis, Corporate Agents organise to alter the parameters in which collective groups are formed and re-formed. In action, whether to reproduce or transform the social system, the outcome affects the original collective categories. The process in which personal morphogenesis anchors the activities of Agency that, consequently, transforms or sustains the collective categories of Corporate and Primary Agents themselves is termed 'double morphogenesis':

> This is 'double morphogenesis' during which Agency, in its attempt to sustain or transform the social system, is inexorably drawn into

sustaining or transforming the categories of Corporate and Primary Agents themselves (Archer 2000: 267).

In an explanatory sense, system outcomes are organically tied to 'double morphogenesis' in the interchange between the choices of persons and the actions of Agency. The outcomes produced from this interchange implicate changes in the array of social roles available and the relationship between these roles. Hence, the Actor's role is anchored in the person vis-à-vis their actions as Agents. The initial role of the Primary Agency is the object of deliberation, which subjects first deliberate upon as part of their constellation of concerns (the first residual problem). The performative enactment of roles is made from this reflexive deliberation and, through Agency, either sustains or transforms society's normativity:

> In living out the initial roles(s), which they have found good reason to occupy, they bring to it or them their singular manner of personifying it or them and this, in turn, has consequences over time. What it does creatively, is to introduce a continuous stream of unscripted role performances, which also over time can cumulatively transform the role expectations. These creative acts are thus transformative of society's very normativity, which is often most clearly spelt out in the norms attaching to specific roles (Archer 2000: 296).

Therefore, as the process of 'double morphogenesis' changes collectives, it also transforms the structure and culture of a society that underpins the roles of social actors. The emergence of social actors is built on the interaction between Primary and Corporate Agents and their outcomes. Consequently, on top of 'double morphogenesis', a 'triple morphogenesis' can occur in which the social identities of Actors are articulated in relation to the actions of agential collectivities. To restate, the actions of these collectivities are anchored in persons and their reflexive capacities:

> In this process, the social identities of individual social actors are forged from agential collectivities in relation to the array of organisational roles which are available in society at that specific time. Both Agents and Actors, however, remain anchored in persons, for neither of the former are constructs or heuristic devices; they concern real people even though they only deal with certain ways of being in society and therefore not with all ways of being human in the world (Archer 1995: 255–256).

As 'triple morphogenesis' transforms society's extant role array (Archer 2000: 295), then the outcomes produced are reflected in systemic parameters that impact the articulation of both Primary and Corporate Agents. Such an increase in the range of roles available means an expanded horizon in which new social movements and interest groups arise (Archer 2000). Hence, the transformation of the socio-structural environment impacts future processes of 'double morphogenesis'. The morphogenetic explanatory problem views the distinction between Social Agent and Social Actor as analytical and temporal. According to Archer, they are not 'different people' but analytically interrelated emergent stratum in which *morphogenetic cycles* — double and triple morphogenesis — mutually impact each other (Archer 2000). This mutual impact is manifested in the interplay between Agency and socio-cultural context — the outcome produced in this morphogenetic process is observed in the emergent properties and characteristics of active roles that condition future Actors.

Rethinking the Morphogenetic Equation by Extending Reflexivity

Internal deliberations are posited as the anchor of Social Agency. The subsequent emergence of the Social Actor depends on the reflexive reasons of selves that personify roles based on their response to the involuntary 'Me'. To posit the anchor of morphogenetic processes in persons is based on the need to defend the transcendent and necessary condition of social life in the continuity of consciousness (Archer 2000). This continuity is the foundation of the emergent personal identity and the properties of humanity that recognise and commit themselves to the social. The anchorage of social life in humanity gives the human-in-the-social irreducible powers to internalise and change society's normativity. As a result, the causal efficacy to change society's normativity is the implication of putting individual reflexivity as the *aprioristic* foundation of social concepts.

This section aims to rethink this morphogenetic equation while maintaining and building on its realist starting point, emphasising a stratified conception of the person. Notably, the re-think positions the transcendental reality of the human-in-the-social as both autonomous and dependent on a stratified social reality. At the same time, primacy is not pre-ascribed to the human-in-the-social; instead, it results from the interactive dynamics of the social relation that anchors personal and socio-cultural morphogenesis. As will be discussed in the coming chapters, the rethinking discussed in this section has implications when extending reflexivity to different levels of sociability. Two key points will be proposed as the basis of a rethink of the previously discussed *morphogenetic paradigm*:

1. Archer neglects the psycho-developmental perspective on reflexivity. While self-regulated practical activity is the foundation and sustains reflexivity, I will argue that reflexive capacity is an emergent stratum of meanings comprised of different developmental selves.

2. Personal reflexivity is not the anchor but an element of social relations. Following the developmental perspective, reflexivity extends to other aspects of social relations and does not need to be ascribed to an individual identity. As collectivities (Agents) can be reflexive in their own right, the Actor can similarly be both individual and collective.

Regarding the first point, continuity of consciousness initiated in practical activity in the material world generates an irreducible trajectory of experiences. The reflexive space between molecules and meanings, according to Archer, generates the earliest concerns navigated by an emergent personal identity. This space makes the enactment of reflexivity irreducible to both the biological bundle of molecules and discursive meanings. The pivotal role of practical world-directed experiences renders speech acts as self-experiences. As reflexivity is made a logical necessity to enact the self-experiences of the individual identity, its developmental dimension is inadvertently neglected.

Indeed, the subjective capacity to reflect on the flow of experiences (the first residual problem) includes practical knowledge of the world. However, this world-directed reflection is an emergent stratum of the initial perspectival ownership of experience — the first personal presence of experience (Zahavi 2013). The perspectival ownership makes the mind/body 'I' perceive itself within the ubiquitous first-personal givenness in the multitude of changing experiences. Thus, the minimal self is between a biological bundle of molecules and discursive meanings. Further, it is the sense of self that unites world-awareness and self-experience. According to Zahavi (2009), the minimal self exists in the subjectivity of experience that is, at the same time, world-directed:

> The minimal self was tentatively defined as the ubiquitous dimension of first-personal givenness in the multitude of changing experiences. On this reading, there is no pure experience-independent self. The minimal self is the very subjectivity of experience and not something that exists independently of the experiential flow. Moreover, the experiences in question are world-directed experiences. They present the world in a certain way, but at the same time they also involve self-presence and hence a subjective point of view. In short, they are of something other than the subject and they are like something for the subject. Thus, the phenomenology of conscious experience is one that emphasises the unity of world-awareness and self-experience (Zahavi 2009: 556).

It is between world-awareness and the minimal self that the subjective/objective interplay unfolds. The capacity to deliberate on changing experiences requires a semantic awareness that is contingent on the lived circumstances of the collective (Primary and Corporate Agency). At the same time, the experiential flow always returns to the bio-physical consciousness (Donati 2011) that provides self-presence with its non-arbitrary direction in personal deliberations.

The interplay between the non-arbitrary and contingent gives personal identity crucial human properties and powers. Moreover, the interplay emphasises the developmental dimension of personal identity through the subjective integration and appropriation of lived experience. The process of subjective integration considers past experience as the sense of self directs itself towards objects. Due to being emergent from differentiated minds/bodies, the genesis of practices is understood through developmental stages that impact how past experiences are filtered when confronting collectivities. It is the genesis of self-present practice, grounded in the process of subjective integration, that disinters human properties and powers from the logic of practices that inhere in collectivities.

The developmental genesis of reflexivity — with its necessary capacities to deliberate on concerns — comprises a continuum of developmental selves. There are five different stages in the development of the conceptual self that make reflexivity possible (Neisser 1988). First, the *ecological self*, appearing in the earliest infancy, is a primitive awareness that the self is practically embedded in its environment and consists of self-regulated bodily interaction with external objects. The awareness of the self in the world (biophysical consciousness) leads to the *interpersonal self*, which extends the ecological self to respond and coordinate its actions with others. Consequently, the self mutually co-perceives objects in its environment. The ecological self and interpersonal self should be viewed as inextricable, since 'awareness of the interpersonal is almost invariably accompanied by a simultaneous awareness of the ecological self.' (Neisser 1988: 395)

The ecological and interpersonal stages represent two aspects of the implicit self from which children develop an implicit (pre-conceptual) self-knowledge that is inherently reciprocal to their environment (Rochat 2001). The *extended self* is memory-based, giving the continuous sense of self a temporal place in the world. It is an autobiographical memory that draws on past experiences as it confronts the present. The extended self appears in childhood — solidified at age three — and gradually takes an important role as individuals grow older. By being able to locate the ecological self through integrating remembered experiences to the present, a life narrative is constructed. The 'I' can look back during present interactions to draw out future behaviour (Neisser 1988: 46).

Later, the *private self* is the stage in which the infant understands its experiences as demarcated from the world, that is, one acquires a sense of exclusivity of his or her experiences. Subjective interiority is introspective and enables the self-concept (the semantic self) by rendering its dedication independent of external circumstances. The private self represents a shift from extrospection to introspection and becomes the basis of the reflexive capacity to deliberate on the world from the first-person perspective. This deliberation facilitates personal planning to achieve personal goals.

The capacity to mentally approximate (reflexivity) represents a shift to the *conceptual self* (Rochat 2010). In the conceptual self, subjective interiority self-consciously integrates its experiences — emergent from practical activity in a biophysical environment — referencing world-directed experiences. The self-conscious attempt to integrate experiences represents a shift to the explicit self that is based on the third-person perspective (public mediation of experience). In this stage, emergent from the implicit self, the explicit self is made possible through others.

Social roles are socio-cultural emergent properties that make possible reciprocal exchanges between the implicit and explicit self.

Personal deliberations that figure in the subject/object interplay (the second residual problem) are possible after developing the conceptual self. In the integration process between the first-person and third-person perspectives, there is the emergence of personal identity. The developmental stages that lead to the conceptual stage, according to Neisser (1988), mean other forms of self-knowledge — the ecological, interpersonal, and private selves — all are represented in the conceptual self:

> Thus our self-concepts typically include ideas about our physical bodies, about interpersonal communication, about what kinds of things we have done in the past and are likely to do in future, and especially about the meaning of our own thoughts and feelings. The result is that each of the other four kinds of self-knowledge is also represented in the conceptual self (Neisser 1988: 54).

The four kinds of self-knowledge are represented in the conceptual self, confirming a stratified conception of personal identity. In each of these selves, distinct variations between individuals impact the development and qualitative enactment of the reflexive capacity and its mental approximations (the conceptual self). Consequently, the unique trajectory of personal morphogenesis is identified in the developmental process — the interplay between the non-arbitrary and contingent — that implicates the logical necessity of an irreducible subjective interiority with its capacity to mentally approximate.

As the temporal interplay between the existential self (the 'I') and its collective context is built on and sustained by different kinds of self-knowledge, the explicit sense of self is not just a public matter. In the emergence of subjective alignment, the process in which mental approximations of world-directed experiences are integrated means there is always an element of loss as it is filtered through the collective context ('Me' and 'We'). The continuity of consciousness means novel experiences require a reflexive imperative in which the non-arbitrary dimension of the self can integrate experiences based on past episodes of personal morphogenesis.

It is the process of 'gain and loss' of experience — the genesis of subjective alignment between the implicit and explicit self — that potentially transforms the personal identity and the role it subsequently adopts (Gallagher and Zahavi 2012). The ability to form self-concepts is developmentally tied to reflexivity, but it can only operate effectively with the existence of mechanisms described above that enable bodily awareness, practical engagement with others, autobiographical memory that draws on past experiences as it confronts the present and the ability to plan practical activities.

Second, as reflexivity is identified with meaning-based deliberation (the formation of self-concepts), then it is possible to extend reflexivity to include any form of meaning-based deliberation that utilises society's conversational meanings.[2] Thus, it is identified with any activity that seeks to manage the outcomes of morphogenetic processes. As Donati observes, reflexivity is a property that extends to other aspects of the social:

> The ambivalence of reflexivity is redefined as a differential property/ability possessed by actors, or networks, or systems with regard to their need for managing the outcomes of morphogenetic processes (Donati 2011).

In the personal management of social identities, the internal conversation manages reciprocal exchanges between the implicit and explicit selves (personal reflexivity). After that, when this personal reflexivity dedicates itself to an explicit self, its powers extend to the activity of collectives.

The interaction between individuals and collectives gives social networks new properties and powers. This extended reflexive process's

---

2   To ensure the efficacy of subjective properties and powers, Archer identifies reflexivity as a property of people (2009). However, when reflexivity is rethought as meanings-based activity, it can take a collective dimension to include the actions of collectives (collective reflexivity of Agency) and the internal dynamics of social networks as social reflexivity. The reciprocal interaction between individuals and Agency impacts the mode of reflexivity of social networks. In turn, the configuration of social networks, considering *morphogenetic cycles*, impacts the reflexive direction of future interactions. Specifically, the sociability sources in these networks — for example, trust, reciprocity, and collaboration — are expressions of interactions that enhance or depreciate social value. Hence, social networks that operate *meta-reflexively* possess their powers through the *relational goods* produced by the actions of Agents and Actors. Consequently, considering the ontology of social networks, social reflexivity is inherently relational as it is enacted mutually through contingently generated reciprocal action that is part of the relationality that constitutes social reality (Donati 2011).

interactive dynamics of sociability result in social reflexivity, the effects of which are seen in socio-cultural structures. Consequently, the social reflexivity of social networks produces relations at the system level wherein direction is an effect of the interactive dynamic between personal, collective, and social reflexivity. An emergent effect is that the system's internal parts are configured by temporal cycles of morphogenetic change. The configuration of elements impacts future patterns of sociability and how the system responds to future interactive dynamics. That system features adapt their operation to the contingencies of interactions is due in part to the inbuilt capability of the system to reflect on itself within the morphogenesis process.[3]

Based on the extension of reflexivity beyond the personal, the anchor of double and triple morphogenesis (the third residual problem) is the interaction between personal reflexivity and the reflexivity of social networks. It is not the relationship between personal reflexivity and collectives that anchors triple morphogenesis. Instead, the dynamic between personal and collective reflexivity within relational networks anchors system outcomes (the properties and array of social roles). Personal reflexivity is an essential element of this interactive dynamic; as a person adopts the role of the Actor (the explicit self), he or she initiates interaction within collectives.

The implications of an extended understanding of reflexivity will be explored in the coming chapters in the context of post-functionalist approaches to education. Specifically, I will look at the design and operation of curriculum and assessment from within reciprocal exchanges of proximity. A system in which actors, networks, and systems are not regulated but enabled to operate *meta-reflexively* valorises the transcendent (the human-in-the-social) dimension of relations. Within

---

3   System characteristics are social mechanisms that are morphogenetic outcomes of reciprocal interactions. As outcomes, they stabilise social networks and conduct future interactions. However, as outcomes of reflexive human activity, they are reflective rather than reflexive. In the case of systemic social mechanisms, reflectivity is the self-referential capability of the system to adapt its characteristics in response to reflexive activity. Reflexivity, on the other hand, is a semantic activity that starts inwards but expands relationally in its operation (Donati 2011). The manner in which the system operates — as a formalised condensation of social networks — is dependent on the properties and modes of reflexivity that exist in the dynamics of sociability from which it is emergent. Therefore, the direction of the system's inbuilt reflective capability is recursively explained by *morphogenetic cycles*.

such a system, fostering the human-in-the-social becomes the purpose of education. Being attuned to the personal in relationships ensures integration starts from making relations reflexive in a transcendental way (Donati 2011). Against the artificial sanctioning of 'excellence', *relational reflexivity* is actuated in practices designed to develop *all* students in response to their unique subjective input points.[4] Thus, input points become the referent, and education practices are evolving referential acts to better understand this referent.

Conclusion

In this chapter, I investigated the question of personhood and the emergence of personal identity. The rationale behind this investigation was to present the *morphogenetic paradigm* that explains the emergence of the human in relation to broader natural, practical, and discursive orders. Thus, to provide an account of this emergence, it is necessary to enter the relational dynamics that generate concerns which need to be navigated by individuals. This means taking the perspective of persons as they deliberate on concerns as part of their developing personal identity. When referential acts proposed as part of policy and practices start from the dynamics of relations that impact the development of the nascent personal identity, they become attuned to the reality of human potentiality. The potentiality of the human is in the development of Personal Emergent Properties (PEP) as part of the morphogenetic trajectory of personal identity.

Both logically and ontologically, conceptually affirming the efficacy of PEP necessitates the primacy of reflexivity in the form of personal deliberations. Reflexivity as a first-person phenomenon is cognitive rather than merely perceptual. Before behaviour is manifested as personal dedication, it is an inward deliberation upon the constellation of concerns emergent from the natural, practical, and discursive orders. The reflexive deliberations of persons — represented in the indexical 'I' — is the transcendentally necessary condition from which dedication

---

4   The student input point refers to the learner's developmental stage at the beginning of a learning cycle. The goal of registering input points is to maintain a coherent learning trajectory for students to ensure vital developmental milestones are not missed before starting the next cycle.

to social roles becomes possible. Based on the input points at different stages of personal *morphogenetic cycles* (the analytical problem), it is possible to account for personal identity's past, present, and future emergence.

As Personal Emergent Properties (PEP) are inherently relational, personal deliberation and subsequent dedication pre-suppose Primary and Corporate Agency. Human capacities logically pre-suppose Agency and the personification of the role of Actor, and double and triple morphogenesis are anchored in reflexive internal conversations. *Morphogenetic cycles* are instigated by changes in personal identity that then generate collective roles leading to the transformation or reproduction of system mechanisms.

This chapter proposed a revision to the *morphogenetic paradigm* that builds on its stratified view of social reality in which structure and Agency intertwine and mutually redefine each other. While still working from the same ontological pre-suppositions, the revision takes a developmental perspective to understand reflexivity and its emergence. Importantly, its revision, taking a developmental perspective, views reflexivity as a discursive capacity that is part of an irreducible trajectory. In this personal trajectory, subjective integration — the unification of self- and world-awareness — is affected by pre-supposing developmental selves. The differentiated way developmental selves produce and sustain the conceptual self (in which reflexivity is enacted) leads to different mental approximations and the first-person presence of world-directed experience.

As reflexivity is viewed as any meaning-based deliberation, it extends to Agency (collective reflexivity) and social networks (social reflexivity). Both collective reflexivity and social reflexivity are pre-supposed by the development of personal reflexivity and the enactment of PEP in the first instance. However, once developed, the management of the morphogenetic process is a reciprocal synergy between levels of the social. It includes relations of proximity to wider networks that impact the reflexive direction of relations. Hence, the interactive dynamics of different levels of reflexivity — personal, collective, and social reflexivity — anchor *morphogenetic cycles*. In a relational order — one that is underpinned by a relational *symbolic code* — the system operates *ex post facto* in response to the noted morphogenetic processes.

The proposed idea of *meta-reflexive* management of morphogenetic processes, which operates within different levels of sociability, is investigated in the coming chapters. What is specifically explored is the idea of a post-functionalist approach to education which starts from developmental input points. It is an inclusive approach to practice and provision that anchors reflexive activity in the interactive dynamics of sociability from which the *latent reality* of the human-in-the-social is emergent. In contrast to the artificial sanctioning of learning that occurs in system-based approaches to credentialing (and neglects developmental input points), the aim is to ensure the potentiality of the human defines the parameters of sociability. If reflexive processes are to operate based on the human/non-human distinction, then practices cannot be static. As a result, an evolving and adaptive *judgmental rationality* is directed at the human-in-the-social.

4. Social Capitalisation & the Making of Relational Goods

In the previous chapter, I discussed the person's emergence through the *morphogenetic paradigm*. The aim of providing this account of personal identity's development was to advocate for a governance model grounded in the relational realist general approach that explains the constitution and development of the *latent reality* of the human. Furthermore, the idea of extending reflexivity — rethought as an emergent meaning-making mechanism — was proposed to include the properties and powers of collectives and networks and their impact on the operation of systems. In this chapter, the vital role of social reflexivity is investigated further. This means exploring the concept of social capital. Social capital names patterns of sociability that enable the generation of emergent relational properties and powers in the form of *relational goods*. It returns to the idea covered in Chapter One of moving beyond modernity's *symbolic code* and its system-based management of environmental contingencies.

Social capital is explored as a form of sociability that differentiates between the human and the social. This distinction is not circular, as it distinguishes between the referential acts (instituted in patterns of sociability) and their desired effect (referencing the *latent reality* of the human element). Notably, the enablement of the subject is central to after-modern formations — the aim is to give responsibility to participants to think and observe relationally to better understand the referent. These transformative patterns of sociability provide the basis for new forms of social capital and *civil society*. The chapter will explore the following two points:

1. Prevailing social capital models are inadequate. After establishing this, I advocate a realist approach that considers the dynamic

patterns of sociability (within morphogenetic cycles) as a dependent and independent variable. The dynamic interplay of social relations connects the agentic and structural elements of social life and, as such, their interaction shapes the outcome of morphogenetic processes (the dynamics of social relations are the object of sociological explanation as they connect the elements that constitute these relations). An emergent civil society is articulated within these processes to ensure patterns of sociability operate humanly.

2. Initiatives that start from the dynamics of the relation seek to transform social reality by exploring the normative connections between the different elements of the relation. Education should be responsive to the needs of individuals, but this can only exist in a morphogenetic relational order wherein identity is underpinned by the relational *symbolic code*. The relational symbolic code normatively guides the relation's orientation and the diverse ways participants respond to each other's needs. It is a relational order that encourages the contribution of participants to enhance its value by enriching the stock of sociability that, in turn, sustains *relational goods*.

Civil Society Starts from the Internal Dynamics of the Social Relation

Genuine learning, I propose, is oriented to the development of the active learner. The activated learner, relationally constituted, develops into the collective subject with transformative properties and powers. This broader view of education means the 'I' is constituted into the 'We' and becomes a *Relational Subject* through properties and powers developed via their social relations:

> The term 'Relational Subject' refers to individual and collective social subjects in that they are *'relationally constituted'*, that is, *inasmuch as they generate emergent properties and powers through their social relations* (Donati & Archer 2015: 58, emphasis original).

Ascribing responsibility to participants to co-create their relations means orienting actions towards the configuration of the relation's elements and the effects they generate. The *Relational Subject* is relationally reflexive when the 'I' identifies as the 'collective subject' whose concerns extend to the relation's 'performance' in achieving its goals (Donati & Archer 2015).

A relation's capacity to facilitate civic values is defined by the system's openness to adapt its performance in reference to the concerns of individual and collective social subjects (the latent dimension of the social relation).[1] An adaptive relational system is one wherein the mode of integration is emergent from morphogenetic processes activated by social subjects within the dynamics of the society in which those subjects are embedded. To enable responsibility is to confer meaning to the relation from the point of view of the human subject that observes and thinks relationally about the latent dimension. *Civil society* is a vision of the 'society of the human' at every level — from system to immediate interactions — in which the reference is the potentiality of the human subject as a *Relational Subject* to produce their society according to the human/non-human distinction:

> From the point of view of the human subject, who has to confer meaning on the relations in which he/she is immersed, this is a new horizon that opens up with the after-modern — the 'society of the human'. The society of the human is that of which it has to be asked, at every level, in every domain, how the latent dimension enters in every social relation and if social processes are operating in a human way or not, in relation to semantics quite different from traditional ones (Donati 2009). The 'society of the human' is not one of many possible worlds, but the distinct world of the human being: it is not a utopian vision of society, but it is the real society as produced according to the human/non-human distinction. To conceptualise this society depends on being able to observe and think relationally (Donati 2011: 166).

Oriented towards such a *civil society*, the proposal here is for an idea of social capital that acknowledges the latent dimension through the actions of those involved. The socio-cultural outcomes are effects of a morphogenetic *civil society* in which sociability is morphogenetically emergent from *relational goods* that produce *Added Social Value (ASV)*. To ascertain if social processes operate humanly, it is conceptually necessary

---

[1] The civic values of social relations are identified in sources of social capital, that is, trust, cooperation, and reciprocity (Donati 2011). When the properties of the relationship develop PEP, that is, are attuned to the relation's performance, then the system becomes adaptive to the concerns of those responsible for the management of its morphogenetic processes. Responsibility implicates better synergy between the civic values of social subjects and the properties of the relationships that they operate within.

to analytically disentangle outcomes (*relational goods*) from their mode of production (sociability) to avoid analytical closure. This necessity is demonstrated in the case of theories of social capital that are shown to evade the internal dynamics of social capitalisation. The implications of this debate are further explored (in the following chapters) in which the reciprocal dynamics of teaching and learning are connected to networked partnerships based on cooperation and trust.

Social Capital Theories Negate the Internal Dynamics of the Social Relation

Prevailing social capital theories neglect the internal dynamics of the relation in different ways. To demonstrate this point, I will consider these three main approaches:

1. Putnam's collective view of social capital as features of social organisation that facilitate action and cooperation for mutual benefit.

2. Coleman's view of social capital as social structures that facilitate individual action and transactions between individuals.

3. Bourdieu's view of social capital as structured modes of subjective regulation.

Putnam's Collective View of Social Capital

Putnam's view of social capital emphasises the importance of a strong and active *civil society* that consolidates democracy (Putnam 1995). In this view, civic engagement, as found in organised reciprocity and civic solidarity networks, is a pre-condition for good governance that can tackle social problems effectively. Putnam thus uses social capital to refer to 'features of social organisation such as networks, norms, and social trust that facilitate coordination and cooperation for mutual benefit' (Putnam 1995: 67). Therefore, social outcomes and the features of social organisation become analytically tied. Dense networks of interaction (networks of civic engagement) replenish the stock of social capital that, in turn, helps cooperation for mutual benefit. For example, social problems are tackled through corporate action. Putnam cites considerable empirical evidence to argue that the efficacy of social organisations is tied to civic engagement because this generates social trust. Social trust and social engagement are strongly correlated, and these two facets are indicative of social capital:

> Across the 35 countries in this survey, social trust and civic engagement are strongly correlated; the greater the density of associational membership in a society, the more trusting its citizens. Trust and engagement are two facets of the same underlying factor — social capital (Putnam 1995: 73).

Hence, generating and expanding the density of associational ties is necessary to sustain social capital. The structure of these associational networks requires forms of social connectedness — restoring civic engagement and civic trust — that are organised horizontally.[2] The horizontally ordered organisation is better equipped to sustain norms of reciprocity that are important for collective action:

> If horizontal networks of civic engagement help participants solve dilemmas of collective action, then the more horizontally structured an organisation, the more it should foster institutional success in the broader community. Membership in horizontally ordered groups (like sports clubs, cooperatives, mutual aid societies, cultural associations, and voluntary unions) should be positively associated with good government (Putnam 1993: 175).

Social Capital as a Resource for both Individual and Collective Action

Coleman similarly highlights the importance of social capital as a resource for individual and collective action. The focus here, however, is on social capital as a background context that facilitates the actions of social actors (individual and corporate) within the social structure (Coleman 1990). The emergence of human capital — that is, the developing of skills and capabilities — depends on social capital being

---

2   Putnam distinguishes between horizontal and vertical associations based on the power balance between agents within networks of interpersonal communication and exchange: 'Any society—modern or traditional, authoritarian or democratic, feudal or capitalist—is characterized by networks of interpersonal communication and exchange, both formal and informal. Some of these networks are primarily "horizontal," bringing together agents of equivalent status and power. Others are primarily "vertical," linking unequal agents in asymmetric relations of hierarchy and dependence.' (Putnam 1993: 173)

utilised in relations between individuals. Social capital is efficacious when it performs a function from the perspective of the individual's purposive action. It is a background resource and a public good that affects those participating in the social structure.

A tension arises between social capital as it benefits an individual and its broader role as a public good and shared resource. To resolve this, the organisational features of social capital become crucial in maintaining its social function as a public good. For example, norms and sanctions that motivate individuals to be self-invested also need shared obligations, expectations, and trust. If this resource is available to all members of a social structure, it is essential to connect individuals to relationships in which social capital is generated. Social capital exists in social structures, and simultaneously, the trustworthiness of social structures proliferates obligations and expectations when it operates effectively and inclusively. Ultimately, social capital is defined by its function — it is an organised social resource that facilitates the purposive action of actors within the social structure (Coleman 1975).

Social Capital as Part of a Broader Field of Practices

Bourdieu views social capital as part of broader fields of practice. In these fields, social capital is a manifestation of power which relationally converges with other types of capital (capital operating as a social relation of power). Transmission of collectively owned capital is understood as membership in a group that provides its members with access to resources. Membership involves ownership of social capital that gives access to other types of capital (resources) through possession of a durable network of institutionalised relationships of mutual acquaintance and recognition:

> Social capital is the aggregate of the actual or potential resources which are linked to possession of a durable network of more or less institutionalised relationships of mutual acquaintance and recognition — or in other words, to membership in a group — which provides each of its members within the backing of the collectively-owned capital, a 'credential' which entitles them to credit, in the various senses of the word (Bourdieu 1986: 21).

In Bourdieu's understanding, social life has subjective and objective dimensions that are linked by the habitus. The social field — the objective dimension — is the configuration of objective relations between positions. The position regulates the subjective dispositionality of its occupant (the habitus) and the reflexive enactment of the occupant's powers in relation to the distinction of 'species of power' (capital) and other occupants in the objective field of relations (Bourdieu 1986). To avoid an accusation of objective reductionism, Bourdieu emphasises that the subjective habitus is internally regulated (he terms this as a subjectively inculcated structuring structure) that makes possible the achievement of infinitely diversified tasks. Therefore, the objective field provides the occupant with schemes allowing the solution of similarly shaped problems — but it is the occupant that integrates these schemes and applies solutions. Thus, Bourdieu defines the habitus in the following way:

> A system of lasting, transposable dispositions which, integrating past experiences, functions at every moment as a matrix of perceptions, appreciations, and actions and makes possible the achievement of infinitely diversified tasks, thanks to analogical transfers of schemes permitting the solution of similarly shaped problems (Bourdieu 1977: 72)

As Lin notes, Bourdieu's theory of social capital falls within the broad category of neo-capital theories that stress the interplay of individual actions and structural positions in the capitalisation process (Lin 2004). Social capital, specifically, in Bourdieu's view, is a form of capital that is connected to group membership and the social networks accessed through this membership. The quality and volume of social capital is a resource that generates (relationally) gains in cultural and economic capital.

Analytical Closure in Social Capital Theories

The theories noted above attempt to articulate an understanding of social capital considering the subjective and objective properties of social life. Each differently considers how, through analytical closure, the interaction between relational elements — whether subjective or objective — is negated. Firstly, Putnam starts from the pre-conditions of good governance and a prosperous economy. As a result, features of social capital, for example, social trust, social norms, and social networks of civic engagement, generate pro-social outcomes in the form of good governance and a prosperous economy.

Starting from the effect to derive the pre-supposing inputs, Putnam's theory does not distinguish features and outcomes. Portes argues that it is circular to utilise the effect of civic virtue to formulate sweeping policy prescriptions. Observed differences are retroactively explained by the prime determinant of civic virtue:

> Tautology in this definition of social capital results from two analytic decisions; first, starting with the effect (i.e., successful cities versus unsuccessful cities) and working retroactively to find out what distinguishes them: second, trying to explain all of the observed differences (Portes 1998: 20).

Lin (2004) and Portes (1998) both note that the objective features of social capital generate different outcomes, that is, the generation of public 'goods' or public 'bads' (Portes 1998: 18). Putnam's focus on the positive and integrative function of rich stocks of social capital neglects possible adverse outcomes caused by the inputs of social capital. For example, social reciprocity — increases in the levels of social capital — can be generated in ways that exclude outsiders and lead to closure and isolation rather than mutual benefit.

Putnam's theory of social capital, starting from outcomes and then working retroactively, bypasses interaction dynamics between the elements of the social relation. Attention to the dynamics is vital because the contingencies of interaction with its observed differences are distinguished from the features of social capital that are subsequently produced (trust, networks of civic engagement, and social norms). Consequently, due to making internal dynamics indistinguishable from outcomes, we have analytical closure as a result of focusing on the organisational features of social capital that regulate the social context of interaction. The objective characteristics of social capital are utilised to explain the observed differences in outcomes.

Hence, the integrative function of rich stocks of social capital (the objective features of social organisation) facilitates coordination and cooperation for mutual benefit and collective well-being. Starting from the inner dynamics of the relation resolves potential problems with tautological definitions of social capital. It does not work retroactively to find optimal regulatory determinants of a public good. We need to account for what produces features of social capital, as I will clarify, in the process of social morphogenesis that explains the origins and development of organisational characteristics (whether transformative or reproductive).

Coleman, on the other hand, sought to emphasise the process of capitalisation for both individual and collective actors. As a social resource for purposive action, the social relations underpinning social capital are understood as an upward conflation from actors to the organisational structures. Social capital functions by supporting the creation of human capital (the development of skills and capabilities). As a result of the tendency to view social capital as a resource for action, Coleman further views it as a public good with obligations if it is to be sustained and used by others. A sense of individual responsibility to the resource used occurs when the social structure works for the user, resulting in mutual interest to support the action structure. Like Putnam, Coleman's theory of social capital renders it a social effect but one that is explained by the preferences of individual and collective actors: the actor uses the resource, and he or she reciprocates the obligation towards social capital as a public good when it fulfils its required (individual) function.

Lastly, Bourdieu views social capital in relation to other types of capital in a struggle to gain power in social fields. His theory's emphasis on the reproductive role of social capital leads to a view of it as a privileged good. Bourdieu acknowledges the necessity of a relational model that understands social reality to exist in things (social fields) and minds (habitus). Yet, he views the habitus as the product of the social world it encounters while taking this world for granted:

> Social reality exists, so to speak, twice, in things and in minds, in fields and in habitus, outside and inside of agents, and when habitus encounters a social world of which it is a product, it finds itself 'as a fish in water', it does not feel the weight of the water and takes the world about itself for granted ... The structuring affinity of habituses belonging to the same class is capable of generating practices that are convergent and objectively orchestrated outside of any collective 'conspiracy' or consciousness. In this fashion it explains many of those phenomenon of quasi-teleology which can be observed in the social world (Bourdieu in Bourdieu & Wacquant 1992: 127).

Finalism is ascribed to the collective social conditions of production of the habitus. Individuals strategise, but personal strategies are regulated in ways pre-given by the environing social world. Once again, like Putnam and Coleman, Bourdieu starts from the effect — in this case, the social constitution of the habitus — and then works backwards to ascertain ways individuals improvise and respond to changes in the same conditions of existence. Bourdieu's model views social practices from the conjuncture between the objective conditions of production of the habitus and the habitus's durable principles that reproduce these same objective conditions:

> The habitus, the durably installed generative principle of regulated improvisations, produces practices which tend to reproduce the regularities immanent in the objective conditions of the production of their generative principle, while adjusting to the demands inscribed as objective personalities in the situation, as defined by the cognitive and motivating structures making up the habitus (Bourdieu 1977: 78).

The result is that the habitus — social history internalized as a component of one's nature — links the objective structure to the social conditions it defines. Bourdieu further denies that the individual may exist in a way independent of the collective history of his or her group or class. An individual habitus is a structural variant of the collective group habitus:

> Since the history of the individual is never anything other than a certain specification of the collective history of his group or class, each individual system of dispositions may be seen as a structural variant of all the other group or class habitus, expressing the difference between trajectories and positions (Bourdieu 1977: 86).

To confirm ontological complicity between the social world that generates the habitus and the individual habitus, Bourdieu introduces the concept of the 'hysteresis effect'. It describes a disjuncture between habitus (in minds) and social context (in things). The disjuncture is caused by a change in a pre-existing context in which the habitus, in the creative enactment of its objective mode of generation, can no longer adapt to the demands of its new context. The interaction between field and habitus is no longer one of complementarity due to, in the words of Bourdieu, a structural lag:

> The hysteresis of habitus, which is inherent in the social conditions of the reproduction of the structures in habitus, is doubtless one of the foundations of the structural lag between opportunities and the dispositions to grasp them which is the cause of missed opportunities and, in particular, of the frequently observed incapacity to think historical crises in categories of perception and thought other than those of the past, albeit a revolutionary past (Bourdieu 1977: 83).

The hysteresis effect refers to a change in the field affecting the ability of the habitus to strategise and make decisions. The earlier habitus is no longer relevant, and the subject needs to adapt to new conditions that arise with changes in the social field. Consequently, the objective conjuncture that regulates the habitus does not fit the new conditions. Therefore, in a historical crisis, the habitus adapts to meet the demands of the new field and conditions of living as social history.

As the hysteresis effect is inherent in the social conditions of reproduction of the habitus structures, we start from these conditions to explain individual systems of dispositions. Subjective disjuncture is presented first from changes in social conditions. Missed opportunities are explained by the incapacity of the individual to generate practices that fit these different conditions:

> Thus, as a result of the hysteresis effect necessarily implied in the logic of the constitution of habitus, practices are always liable to incur negative sanctions when the environment with which they are actually confronted is too distant from that to which they are objectively fitted (Bourdieu 1977: 78).

Bourdieu starts from social capital effects. These, as part of a system of lasting, transposable dispositions integrating past experiences, mean that subjective relations are regulated to produce perception and thought that align with existing categories. Consequently, it is unclear how the collective is transmitted and inculcated to generate subjective alignment. Accordingly, social capital is conceived in his theory as an exchanged credit in relation to other forms of capital that are part of a broader field that regulates action. It is developed as part of an objective fit to a group or class habitus. What is missing from this conception is the singularity of the human person that actively deliberates on his or her social context. Bourdieu's sociology starts from the impersonal properties of the environment that, in collaboration, generates the logic and constitution of the habitus.

The analytical shortcomings in Putnam's, Coleman's, and Bourdieu's approaches to social capital show the necessity of starting from the dynamics of the social relation. As noted in Chapter Three, relational realism is a general sociological approach (a *philosophical ontology*) that answers substantive questions in analytically inclusive terms, that is, all elements are acknowledged, and their relationality shapes the direction of sociability. Its explanatory potential is greater as it first articulates the internal properties of the relation and, after that, arrives at its effects. The inclusivity of relational realism answers all four sociological questions.[3] It explicitly addresses the fourth (normative) question in referential detachment to the human element. The question 'what is to be done?' necessitates an epistemic awareness — that is, reflexivity — about the trajectory of social relations and the outcomes they produce. The normative question judges the internal effects of the relation and the outcomes they produce (Donati & Archer 2015).

A Morphogenetic View of Social Capital

In this section, I propose the idea of sociability as an irreducible process that impacts social capital renewal.[4] The approaches to social capital discussed above demonstrated temporal circularity and analytical closure when starting from an individualist or holistic starting point, whereas the morphogenetic notion of sociability denotes actions based on the relational reference and ties expressed in interactions (Donati 2011).[5] Directed by the relational *symbolic code*, the reciprocity of those in relation generates contextual resources (sources of social capital) in

---

3   The four questions being: (1) where have we come from? (2) what is it like now (3) where is it going? And (4) what is to be done? (Donati & Archer 2015).
4   The process of social capitalisation (generation of relational goods) is a morphogenetic one that analytically starts from existing relations of sociability and its reflexive mediation by *Relational Subjects*. From a relational realist perspective, social capitalisation enables social subjects to utilise existing sources of social capital to renew the fabric of sociability to produce future relational goods.
5   In the theories noted before, there was a view of social capital as virtuous collective civic-mindedness (Putnam), a subjective public resource (Coleman), and a system-based form of capital that regulates the field of individual practices (Bourdieu).

the form of trust, cooperation, and reciprocity. As these are produced in reciprocal exchanges, contextual resources augment the fabric of sociability, building *relational goods*.

Sociability, considering its effects, is both a dependent and independent variable. First, the fabric of sociability configured to generate pro-social values — that is, a virtuous cycle producing *ASV* (*Added Social Value*) — activates *Relational Subjects* to produce *relational goods* cooperatively. As a result, in a relational mode of production, the *relational goods* produced are necessary for the re-generation of *ASV* that makes other *relational goods*.

In contrast to reductionist social capital explanations, to consider sociability as a dependent and independent variable yields a stratified and morphogenetic understanding of *relational goods* as both *explanans* and *explanandum* of sociability (Donati & Archer 2015). The sources of sociability (*ASV*) are emergent from relations of sociability, and these explain the origins and trajectory of *relational goods*. Whether outcomes are *explanans* or *explanandum* is dependent on the temporal phase of morphogenesis and the input of elements in particular phases:

> The recursiveness between sociability (SY) and relational goods (RG) is only apparent in the sense that it can be resolved by introducing the morphogenetic scheme, which takes into account the temporal phases and the autonomous ('stratified') input of every element in the process's particular phases (Donati & Archer 2015: 308).

When outlining the dynamics of this process, the elements are posited as distinct kinds of emergent properties. They are, though ontologically distinct, encountered conjointly (Archer 2011). Sociability and *Relational Subjects* are two realities that are temporally generated and re-generated in dialogue with each other (see Figure 5).

T1– Starting network: there exists (or is formed *ex novo*) a network of relations among actors that is activated/mobilized to produce a service (it is the design of a social intervention), which hypothesizes the creation of a relational good

↘ SY as dependent variable (*explanandum*)

T2– Interactions in the network: the dynamic of the network of relations generates more or less reflexive interactions (that produce or consume SY) –T3

↘ SY as independent variable (*explanans*)

T4– Properties of the emergent network and its effects: the SY emerging from the interactions in the network produces the service planned at the beginning as a relational good (the social intervention is successful), or it does not realize it or achieves it only in part (the social intervention fails or is partial)

TIME

Fig. 5 Added social value of sociability (SY) as the re-generation of relational goods (RG) over time (cycle T1–T4), that is, as alteration of the order of relations through the order of interactions (Donati & Archer 2015: 309).

The morphogenetic scheme uncovers the origins of *relational goods* through the internal properties of relations of production and the autonomous (stratified) input of elements in these relations.

Emergent Realities of Sociability

The interdependence between relations of production and the production of relational goods considers three emergent realities of sociability:

1. The subject as a person.
2. Structure/culture as objective realities.
3. The features of social relationships bind subjective and objective elements into enduring arrangements.

The interplay of these realities within the context of the social relation reveals the origin of the relation and *how* and *why* it was produced:

In practice, this means that specific accounts are required to explain how particular parts of the social order originated and came to stand in a given relationship to one another, *whose* actions were responsible for this, through which interactions, *when* and *where* and with *what* consequences. In all of this, the practising sociologist has to know a great deal about the historical origins and current operations of 'x' (Archer 2011: 59, emphasis original).

To make the morphogenetic processes tractable for investigation, Archer (2011) breaks up the flow of events into three phases: Structural conditioning (T1) → Social interaction (T2–T3) → Structural elaboration (T4). These phases aim to account for the origins of the structure by moving backwards from effects — the current operations of 'x' — to the activity of agents and the structural conditions they initially face. The activity dependence of social order produces diachronic or synchronic outcomes that are explained by the actions of those responsible for its operation and the effects of their social activity. Morphogenetic processes account for what happens in pursuing reproduction or transformation and *why* specific agents were motivated to adopt certain directions vis-à-vis the social relation (see Figure 6).

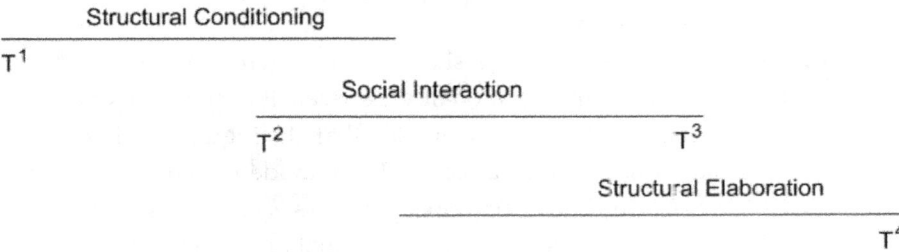

Fig. 6 The basic morphogenetic sequence (Archer 2011: 62).

In the morphogenetic explanatory framework, the effects of the social relation at T4 include the efficacious actions of Agency that potentially transcends the objective regulation of the subject (Chapter Three covered this process in the case of double and triple morphogenesis). Therefore, the emergence of corporate actors is part of a process defined within the dynamics and interplay of the social relation. The emergence of Agency's 'We' impacts personal identity and society's normativity, which underpins social identity.

Adopting a relational view on *how* and *why* sociability and *relational goods* are produced — depending on the morphogenetic stage analysed — leads to inclusive explanations about what can be done to generate *ASV* that creates future valuable *relational goods*. Hence, the fourth normative question of sociology cannot be adequately answered unless the origins of relations of production are considered. Only the *meta-reflexive* input of the corporate 'We' — the *Relational Subject* — can reflexively steer the different levels of sociability to generate innovative emergent properties and powers through their social relations. The emergent properties that are generated increase the parameters of sociability — growing the social value of those in relation — from which *relational goods* are produced. Against individualist and holist views of social capital, the relationality that produces sociability is the starting point of an emergent *civil society* beyond system-based governance models.

The Morphogenetic Paradigm and Civil Society

A *civil society* that transcends modernity's functionalist integration model affirms education service as a post hoc emergent function of the relation's finalism.[6] Hence, the reference of the relation (the finalism that guides its renewal) is the shared orientation ('We-ness') that normatively regulates the relationality between its internal elements and their effects. The two characteristics that distinguish *civil society* are a relational ethicality and a *meta-reflexive* mode of reflexivity that extends to persons and social networks. I discuss each of these in turn.

Relational ethicality arises from the relational realist epistemological approach insofar as the latter starts from the processes of interaction to answer the fourth normative question, that is, how referential judgement on practices meet the needs of persons within their relationality. Relational realism, starting from the historical origins of relations (its social causes), embeds the reference of ethicality within pre-existing relational configurations and the outcomes they produce. Instead of the holism of impersonal structures or individual preferences, the

---

6   The relation's finalism is in its *symbolic reference* (its 'We-ness') shaped by the latent reality of the human-in-the-social.

outcomes sought are situated and relationally emergent. Accordingly, the *Relational Subject* is orientated towards the relational value of the good (Donati & Archer 2015). The relational nature of the good sought exists in the *ASV* generated that extends the parameters of sociability. The relations of production (an objective reality) establish the relational nature of the good sought.

The meta-reflexive mode of reflexivity extends to persons and social networks in relational realism. Because of the interdependence between sociability and relational goods, generation and re-generation of the latter requires *meta-reflexive* management of the relationship between *primary, secondary, and generalised sociability* (the relational mode of production). Specifically, the *meta-reflexive* management of relations requires *Relational Subjects* capable of assessing the capacity of networks to produce *relational goods* that expand the parameters of sociability synergistically. Rather than regulated reproduction, innovation necessitates *meta-reflexive* management of relations at all levels of society. In *civil society*, the *common good* is generated by outward-looking subjects that co-create an identity that exceeds the relation's aggregate elements. Synergistically integrating these elements is fundamental to producing a renewed fabric of sociability whose associational structures further the *common good*.

In relational ethicality, *judgemental rationality* (the normative question) enacts via *meta-reflexivity* the processes of social capitalisation that produce *ASV*. Each morphogenetic phase articulates social capitalisation in these processes by disentangling sociability from its outcomes.[7] In the temporal interplay of inputs, vis-à-vis double and triple morphogenesis, sociability is both the *explanans* and *explanandum* — it is the temporal phase that identifies which aspect of sociability is investigated.

Hence, expanding the horizons of sociability is an outcome of *meta-reflexive* inputs that effectively produce *ASV* by cyclically renewing relational goods. Relational goods are defined not only in the manner they are consumed but also sustained as transformative sources of future cycles of morphogenesis by those active in their formation. The following two chapters explore the notion of *civil society* in the context

---

7   Each phase includes the relational inputs of personal, collective, and social reflexivity.

of teaching and learning. The *common good* that gives identity and direction to education is talent development, which, in turn, enables the generation of *Relational Subjects*. Practices are proposed and enacted in reciprocal connections between teachers and students. The situated nature of learning references the autonomous input point of students at the beginning of learning cycles. These evolving input points are then transformed within partnerships to produce relational goods that morphogenetically shift the horizons of sociability.

Concluding Remarks

In this chapter, I extended and applied a relational realist *philosophical ontology* (observing and thinking relationally, in a substantive sense) to the idea of *civil society*. *Civil society* starts from the perspective of the human subject, which entails a conferral of meaning to relations based on the human/non-human distinction. The human perspective becomes the *latent reality* of social relations whose parameters require *meta-reflexive* management that is inherently transformative. In turn, this *civil society* depends on civic values that are the source of *ASV* needed to sustain the transformative parameters of sociability through the actions of *Relational Subjects*.

In providing an account of a sustainable *civil society*, I presented an alternative theory of the process of social capitalisation (the making and re-making of the reality of sociability). The prevailing social capital theories reviewed in this chapter show analytical closure in different ways, analysing the dynamics of sociability through the prism of individual or holistic elements of relations. First, Putnam does not distinguish between organisational features and their outcomes. As a result, we are left with circularity with the integrative function of rich stocks of social capital — that is, the process of social capitalisation — made indistinguishable from the effects they produce.

Coleman understands the effects of social capital as relationally embedded utilitarian resources that are part of the preference schedule of individual and collective actors. In this form of utilitarian contractualism, social capital becomes a reciprocated investment in which the sharing of resources depends on trust developed from the cost/benefit experiences of actors (Coleman 1998). Coleman considers social capital to consist of relations between persons, but how efficacious these relations are at maintaining public goods is referenced from the actor's perspective. He or she must first perceive the benefits of social capital as a good worthy of reciprocating, that is, bringing into being for others to use, too. Formal organisation is needed to overcome problems arising in the supply of public goods resulting from the possible disinterest of actors in collectively generating these goods. Forms of social capital — obligation and expectations (dependent on trustworthiness), the information-flow capability of the social structure, and norms accompanied by sanctions — are embodied in social structures to achieve strong relationships. Again, the goal is to provide benefits from the perspective of actors:

> Social relations and social structures facilitate some forms of social capital; actors establish relations purposefully and continue them when they continue to provide benefits (Coleman 1988: 105).

In Bourdieu's theory, which also posits a system perspective as the starting referent, social capital is understood to be in a struggle with other types of capital to gain power in social fields. There is a reproductive focus on social capital as a privileged good. The individual is inseparable from the collective history of her group or class (ontological complicity). Social capital, thus, is configured with other types of capital — in a field of practice — in which the habitus is a structural variant of the collective group habitus.

The limitations of these different theories of social capital demonstrate the need for an alternative approach capable of opening analytical pathways. It is vital to disentangle the process of social capitalisation to ensure that the relation is the analytical starting point. In relation, the human element is co-emergent as it is it is also active in conferring meaning to the patterns of sociability. The *Relational Subject*, in enabling responsibility to make and re-make the fabric of sociability, mediates between relational goods and the renewal of this same fabric. Depending on the morphogenetic stage — in which relational goods are both *explanans* and *explanandum* — the *ASV* produced by *Relational Subjects* sustains future cycles and the enhancement of their conditions of production. Sociability and relational goods are two realities that are temporally generated and re-generated in dialogue with each other (Archer 2011).

To explain the origins of the social capitalisation process, it is necessary to acknowledge the different input points of sociability, including subjective actors, socio-cultural realities, and the organisational features of relationships that bind the subjective and objective features. As mediators, the *Relational Subject* (individual or collective) is part of the *meta-reflexive* management of the relation within ties expressed through observing and thinking relationally. The *meta-reflexive* management of the social capitalisation process consists of facilitating synergy between personal, collective, and social reflexivity. The outcomes produced by this synergistic form of relational goods are continuously worked on through changing conditions that further enable the *Relational Subject*.

By disentangling the process of social capitalisation, the notion of *civil society* provides context to teaching and learning. The reference point, when starting from the human perspective, is the student's development that is constituted in personal morphogenetic inputs points at the beginning of each learning cycle. It is necessary to think of the student as an autonomous learner but also as a potential *Relational Subject* who takes part in the noted synergistic process that underlies all levels of society. In *civil society*, the mission of education is the development of both of these facets of the individual in the broader context of relational ethicality. This relational ethicality is emergent from the morphogenetic dialogue between sociability and relational goods. Between sociability and relational goods, the aim is to continuously enable potential personal capabilities that confer meaning to relations through a relational mode of observation enacted by *Relational Subjects*.

5. Student Development as the Referential Reality of Education

This chapter proposes an alternative education service based on the relational realist approach. I aim to show how it can lead to an alternative value horizon and different practices by institutional organisation on the level of face-to-face interactions. In presenting this case, the chapter is divided into two main areas that are inter-related and establish an alternative to system-based *lib/lab* approaches:

1. A relational epistemology that starts from the ontology of the relation is applied to Parsons's AGIL functional model.[1] The goal is to utilise this model in a relational way in which the value-pattern (L) of the model is deemed emergent from the relation, that is, its *symbolic reference*. In a relational epistemic approach, the evolutionary relationship between observer and observed connects the learner to the schooling environment from the learner's perspective (the value-pattern of the relation).

2. The hegemony of the *lib/lab* model in education compromises learners' autonomy and, thus, the potential development of all students. Employability is the dominant rationale that informs education policies and practices. In this context, the parameters of learner needs are derived from an external mode of determination

---

1   The AGIL scheme is appropriated in a way that moves from Parsons's emphasis on the functionalist prerequisites of an institutionalised system of action to an analytic compass that coheres with a stratified and emergent understanding of social reality. In the case of the relational understanding of social reality, relations consist of four orientations of meaning – means (A), goals (G), norms (I) and values (L). The relationality of these four dimensions analytically accounts for the emergence of social facts. Hence the fundamental point of reference when accounting for the emergence of social facts is not the norms of integration of environmental interchanges – as is the case in Parsons's AGIL – but the reciprocal interaction between the dimensions of social relations (Donati 2011).

— the complex and changing needs of the economy. This extrinsic definition of education's parameters influences curriculum planning, assessment design, and learners' credentialing. The learner is a human capital resource whose skills are pre-directed in an up-down centralised outcome-based approach to sociability. While system-based large-scale group testing screens and categorises students into graded bands, the relational alternative starts from reciprocity that buttresses the learner's agency in the learning process. The learning environment, when defined by its relationships, is understood as the place of emergence of value patterns that guide the nature of ties that bind reciprocally oriented subjects.

Talent Development is Education's Referential Reality

The realist *philosophical ontology* considers the nature of social reality and emphasises the interplay within relationships that generate this reality. It starts from the premise, discussed in earlier chapters, that social reality is relational, that is, the relation is not derived from pre-identified elements but is a *sui generis* emergent reality. From this perspective, we differentiate the human (*refero*) and the interconnectedness of the human to the socio-cultural context. Relational education, in admitting these previously discussed preliminaries, derives its legitimacy from the capabilities of those involved to transform their environment in ways that acknowledge this interconnectedness in reference to the transcendental dimension that defines the function of social roles, whether at the institutional level or within the classroom. In this context, talent development — that is, the development of the human element — is education's relational orientation and referential object. The epistemic quadrangle, discussed in Chapter Two, is a knowledge approach enacted, in contrast to system-based models, from within the relationality of learning environments to advance its referential object (*latent reality*). The approach links personal morphogenesis to the socio-culture context of education provision (social morphogenesis).

The referential detachment of the epistemic quadrangle means a reciprocal orientation of subjects-in-relation that directs transformative social formations and practices. In the case of education practice, the model describes how the ontological reality of the learner is represented and responded to within relationships. Responsive practices judge the efficacy of education practices according to how the relative autonomy of the student — as a concrete singularity — is directed from within a socio-cultural context. Accordingly, the relational *symbolic code* of the socio-cultural context ties the teacher to the learner and recognises three main concerns in education:

1. The teacher is in referential detachment to the learner's reality as Alter (the learner as a concrete singularity).

2. The socio-cultural context mediates the epistemic relation between *Ego and Alter*. Social reflexivity, through reciprocal partnerships, transforms this context to maximise talent development. As required outcomes morphogenetically return to the reflexive interplay within relationships, the parameters of sociability need to be expanded to produce relational goods that further the efficacy of learner development. Thus, the *relational goods* generated produce Added Social *Value* (ASV) in the form of innovative practices that further learning efficacy. Talent development then becomes a relational good sustained by ASV that extends to other social domains and is part of broader societal reflexivity within a synergy of interconnected networks.

3. Based on an in-gear conception, which will be discussed in the next chapter, the development of learner agency does not equate to an individualistic notion of learning and knowing (Freire in dialogue with Shor 1987: 99). Learning and knowing are necessary components of a single dialogic undertaking due to the emergence of the human person in and from relational contexts. Consequently, personal emergence means autonomy is relative to the context that provides meaning and direction.

Re-Thinking Parsons's AGIL Functional Scheme in a Relational Way

This section will re-think the AGIL scheme utilising the relational general approach. The significance of the AGIL functional scheme is that it is grounded in modernity's *symbolic code* and is present in the representation of the social in the *lib/lab* approach to policy. First, before proposing a relational re-think of this scheme, it is necessary to outline the theory and its problems briefly. The issues shown will become the basis of the noted relational re-think of Parsons's AGIL scheme.

An Outline of Parsons's *AGIL Scheme*

Parsons sought to abstract the underlying mechanisms that produce uniformities at the level of interactional dynamics. The observed uniformities are generated by the integrative role of normative expectations, institutionalised in social relationships, which individual actors then internalise. This functionalist model aims to posit a relational interconnection between social systems and personalities through reciprocated expectations that are simultaneously objects of the situation. The fundamental starting point is the structure of relations between the involved actors in the interactive process:

> Since a social system is a system of processes of interaction between actors, it is the structure of relations between the actors involved in the interactive process which is essentially the structure of the social system (Parsons 2005: 15).

Signs and symbols are aspects of pattern-maintenance that define the standards reciprocated between actors. These standards are the basis of the relationship's organisation, considering the broader institutionalised environment. Shared expectations (uniformities), therefore, define empirically significant sociological problems. While differentiated capacities or abilities of actors exist, they are not primary determinations of social systems:

> There are differentiated capacities or abilities but for the general population parsimony may be applied. It is relatively unlikely that large-scale social systems are primarily determined by biological differences in the capabilities of populations (Parsons 2005: 5).

The analysis of subjective motivation thus alludes to a broader problem of integration into the cultural system that shapes reciprocated expectations. The problem of integration, for Parsons, is the fundamental relationship common to all types and modes of interactional orientation (Parsons 2005: 7). Value-orientations formulate which aspects of the cultural tradition are articulated in the action system and form part of the motivational mechanisms of individual actors.

As a result, the structure of social systems and their motivational mechanisms objectively exist on an independent level to the personality system. Within the structure of the action frame of reference, with its value-orientation, it is possible to analyse the connection between the personality system and social system. Successful integration between personality and social systems generates a functioning societal system that meets the prerequisites of maintaining the system's longevity. Thus, the processes within the action frame of reference — the conditions of interaction as analytical objects — structure the relations between actors. The system is a network of such relationships.

With their institutionalised relationships, social systems need motivated individuals to fulfil their given status-role. In the relations between actors, the status-role connects the personality system to the structure of relations. Parsons distinguishes the social actor (a bundle of statuses and roles) from the personality system. The structure of relations exists independently and provides motivational mechanisms for individuals to take up conveyed bundles of statuses and roles. The conformity of the personality system to a distinct status-role is mutually interdependent on the motivational mechanisms of the social structures of relations.

The personality system needs to participate actively to maintain the structure of relations, and the structures themselves need to adapt to meet the needs of individuals. Adequate mechanisms are necessary to ensure individuals are motivated to meet personal needs through pre-given status-roles and thus perform their required 'maintenance patterns'. Accordingly, status-roles are constituted by a dynamic interchange between the personality system, cultural system, and the broader structures of relations in the social system. According to Parsons, the integration of the personality system, through the internalisation of common value patterns, is the 'major point of reference for all analysis which may claim to be a dynamic process of social analysis' (Parsons 2005: 27). Personality and social systems, though distinct levels in the dynamics of mutual interchange, are made up of the same 'stuff' (Parsons 2005: 11). Both levels require adequate interchanges to function effectively.

In this analysis, the AGIL functional approach to the personality and social systems emphasises alignment and the glue that generates this alignment is found in the cultural system's value-patterns. These value-patterns align the need-dispositions of the personality and the role-expectations of the social system:

> We know certain fundamental relations between the institutionalisation and the internalisation of culture. Above all, perhaps, we know that the fundamental common sector of personalities and social systems consists in the value-patterns which define role-expectations. The motivational structures thus organised are units both of personality as a system and of the social system in which the actor participates; they are need-dispositions of the personality and they are role-expectations of the social system (Parsons 2005: 363).

The relationship between the need-dispositions of the personality, role-expectations of the social system, and internalised-institutionalised value-patterns of culture organises action systems. Managing the organism's relationship by considering role expectations and value-patterns defines the system of action as a boundary-maintaining system.[2] The relationship of the need-dispositions is, therefore, understood in terms of its interdependence on its environment:

> This fundamental relationship between need-dispositions of the personality, role-expectations of the social system and internalised-institutionalised value-patterns of the culture, is the fundamental nodal point of the organisation of systems of action. It is the point at which both the interdependence and the independence from each other of personality, social system and culture focus (Parsons 2005: 363).

The systems of action are viewed from the perspective of structured relationships. Thus, the personality system works parallel to the AGIL of the social system with regard to the institutionalisation of value-patterns. It is the value-pattern that regulates the personality system's subjective orientation and goal-directed behaviour. For this reason, the role-status of the social system should be adequately responsive to the need-dispositions of personalities. To sustain motivational structures is, simultaneously, to fulfil social system needs.

---

2   A system of action refers to relations between interdependent organisms and non-social objects within a shared environment. The organism's system of relations to its environment is the frame of reference of a system of action: 'It is this relational system which is the system of action, not the organism as a system' (Parsons 2005: 364). As the system of action is identified as relational, its interchanges with the environment implicate boundary-maintaining processes to distinguish it as an organism. Parsons terms the system as boundary-maintaining through 'certain constancies of pattern' (Parsons 2005: 324) that establish a fundamental point of reference for analysing its environmental interchanges.

Parsons states this relationship between individual and system needs in terms of status-roles that connect the institutionalisation of value-patterns with their internalisation at the personality level. The dyadic relationship of *Ego and Alter* is aligned through roles that integrate the personality system into a social system. It is the *system* of interaction as a collectivity with its roles that pre-suppose the process of interaction through norms regulated through common values.[3] Parsons writes,

> As personalities, each individual may be considered a system with its own values, goals, etc., facing the other as part of an 'environment' that provides certain opportunities for goal-attainment as well as certain limitations and sources of frustrations. Though interdependence can be taken into account at this level, this isn't equivalent to treating the process of interaction as a social system. True, the action of alter is an essential part of the conditions bearing on the attainment of ego's goals, but the vital sociological question concerns the nature and degree of the integration of the *system* of interaction as a social system (Parsons 1985: 164).

Transcending System-Based Value-Patterns

Parsons's analysis of dynamic processes starts from the integration of interchanges between the personality system, the cultural system, and the broader structure of relations that make up the social system. What is the rationale that defines this dynamic process? It is the perspective of institutionalised value-patterns and the normative integration of the personality system into these value-patterns. Parsons's framework resonates with modernity's *symbolic code* insofar as it aims to provide enough space for individuals to identify their needs but regulates the environment, which determines the agreed-upon reciprocal interchanges. The relational autonomy of the personality system is pre-defined in the context of this system-based structured dialectic of freedom and control.

---

3   Collectivity, according to Parsons, is a 'system of concretely interactive specific roles'. Thus, collectivity is more specific than institutions and refers to particular systems of interaction. Institutions, on the other hand, organise roles through a 'complex of patterned elements in role expectations which may apply to an indefinite number of collectivity' (Parsons 2005: 25). Rather than being context-specific, institutions refer to the fundamental functional problem of organising role expectations through normative patterns (Johnson 2008).

With its focus on adaptation and reproduction of the normative foundation, Parsons's AGIL of the social relation is a salient feature of *lib/lab* governance and its never-ending goal to integrate the personality system. Governance does not aim to know and develop Alter; instead, it seeks to regulate the relationship with Ego and sustain system performance by adaptation through further functional differentiation. As discussed in previous chapters, this direction in governance attempts to maintain outcomes through mechanisms that seek to motivate and direct subjective orientation. The insular system-based approach of *lib/lab* governance negates the learner's *latent reality*. This negation compromises the utilisation of contextual resources, including organisational settings, when innovating learner-based concepts and practices. To start from the structure of the social relation is to compromise the autonomy of participants. What is needed instead are associational formations to direct education to better meet the needs of learners as irreducible agents and co-creators of their learning.

The epistemology of relational realist sociology re-works the AGIL scheme so that the autonomy of agents in education — whether personal or collective — is translated into concepts and practices that start from the supra-functional (latent) dimension of the relation[4]. The mediation between the observer and this supra-functional dimension is reflexive as the concepts and practices developed within relations are emergent from reconstitutive *morphogenetic cycles*. These cycles continuously transform previously emergent outcomes. Reflexive mediations — seeking to know rather than to regulate — manage the boundaries between *refero* and *religo* within the 'black box' of sociability. Both *refero* and *religo* represent different components of the social relation's AGIL. (L) and (G) identify the model's referential axis (*refero*), while (A) and (I) identify its organisational axis (*religo*) — see Figure 7.

---

4   The supra-functional denotes the activity of individuals or collectives oriented toward the performative dynamics of the relation and the outcomes they produce. It is within and through relations that the human element is co-emergent (the *latent reality*). Hence, the supra-functional is in opposition to the functional model of differentiation that continuously aims to align the need-dispositions of the personality and the role-expectations of the social system (Donati 2011).

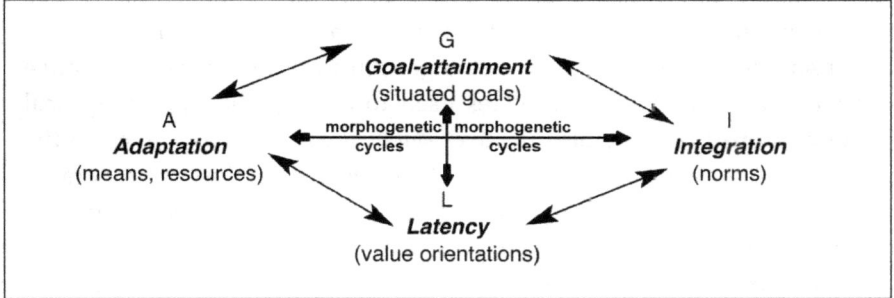

Fig. 7 The components of social relations according to the AGIL scheme (Donati 2011: 87). The diagram has been adapted to show the interchange between the referential (L-I) and organisational (A-G) dimensions of social relations in the context of the morphogenetic emergence of *relational goods*.

Reciprocal and reflexive management of boundaries means the regulated passive subject of system-based functionalism is replaced with an active one given license within the internal dynamics of the relation to co-manage his/her relationality. The reciprocal management of relational differentiation between *Ego and Alter* deepens social inclusion and produces *Added Social Value* (*ASV*). In turn, this *ASV* does not address functional needs but, rather, enhances the sources of social capital (trust, cooperation, and reciprocity) that expand the parameters of sociability. A relational re-thinking of the AGIL scheme replaces the question of integration with a non-system-defined reflexivity from which *relational goods*, producing *ASV*, are generated.

To reiterate, the reflexive imperative within the relation implicates a reflective system that is responsive to the different needs of its participants (*Relational Subjects*). When participants are active, they can redraw the system using the powers and relational autonomy of the personal and collective. Reflexivity also means autonomy to know the latent dimension — the epistemic quadrangle's reference being the normative foundation of the relational *symbolic code* — and, through dialogue (non-negation of Alter), adopts a *meta-reflexive* stance that goes beyond pre-defined value-horizons. The relation's components are related through the reflexive imperative, whose symbolic identity is grounded in the relational epistemological approach.

A relational model, then, does not make interventions that seek to enhance the efficacy of system-defined motivational mechanisms; rather, it ascribes the responsibility of integration to the reflexive imperative that discerns and then dedicates itself to making the right reciprocal connections that generate effective *relational goods*. As explained in the previous chapter, the context in which *relational goods* are generated is the cyclical relationship between the parameters of sociability and *relational goods*, that is, *relational goods* are generated by the environment of sociability, and the parameters of sociability are renewed by the generation of *relational goods*.

Based on the above, a relational rethinking of AGIL raises the following points that impact the organisation and identity of education services. Each of these will be further expanded:

1. Social integration is emergent from the relationality of the different elements of the relation. The referential axis (transcendence) shapes the direction and dynamics of organisational ties that produce this integration (*religo*).

2. As discussed in Chapter Four, the referential axis of AGIL is enacted inside the dynamics of interaction. Integration based on interactive processes means relational concepts and practices must be established to achieve this integration. There is no *a priori* definition of pedagogy or pedagogical outcomes that achieve pre-defined motivational mechanisms for learning. Instead, outcomes follow *ex-post facto* and are based on the inner dynamics of the learning environment. Education takes its fullest sense when the interactive dynamics of learning are the basis of curriculum planning and assessment. The learner takes an active role in directing his or her learning and how subject content is delivered.

3. The relational nature of cognitive processes discussed previously implicates a dialogical conception of the curriculum and learning connected to the world. This conception — the basis of a realist theory of education but also of knowledge — is necessarily interactive. Thus, considering the path of personal morphogenesis, each student has a unique trajectory that is embodied and necessarily develops in dialogue with the world.

Continuity between Primary and Secondary Relational Goods

As stated, relational social integration is normatively shaped by the referential axis (the 'We-ness' of the relation). The referential axis consists of the latency dimension (L) and goals pursued (G). Goals pursued are informed by a reciprocal exchange between interactants guided by their relation's *latent ontological reality* (L). Hence, the social system adapts morphogenetically to change its direction to integrate (I) and meet the needs of its diverse participants in a relationally inclusive manner. The generation of *primary and secondary relational goods* is necessary to maintain synergy and continuity between the referential and organisational dimensions of AGIL.[5]

Primary *relational goods* pertain to networks of proximity that facilitate intersubjective interactions in informal settings, while secondary *relational goods* refer to the formal associative features of networks that extend beyond the familiarity of face-to-face interactions (Donati & Archer 2015). The associative nature of secondary *relational goods* means they play an impersonal organisational role that manages differentiation in immediate primary relations based on the relation's greater identity (its 'We-ness'). The continuity between the subjective, intersubjective, and impersonal dimensions of the relation — correlates with the referential and structural axis of AGIL — shapes the patterns of sociability. These patterns are the *ASV* produced within the parameters of sociability and the renewal of *relational goods* that are subsequently generated in *morphogenetic cycles*.

As noted in the previous chapter, sociability is defined as social relationality in which people's trust and cooperation are acted in the context of a *symbolic reference* ('We-ness') emergent from reciprocal

---

5   The primary *Relational Subject* operates within informal face-to-face interactions. On the other hand, secondary *Relational Subjects* operate within formal social networks that organise informal relations in transformative ways. The weaving of both through the generation of *relational goods* enhances the capacity of *Relational Subjects* to produce further primary and secondary *relational goods*. As a result, there is mutual reinforcement between the activities of primary and secondary *Relational Subjects* that generate *relational goods* in informal face-to-face interactions and in the more organised associations of social solidarity that formalise immediate interactions (Archer & Donati 2015).

interactions and connections. The reflexive transformation of the parameters of this sociability develops collective subjects (Donati 2011). Consequently, the organisational elements of the relation are in dialogue with the interactive dynamics that generate the experiences and practices of teachers and students. The features of these organisational elements encourage classroom teaching and assessment practices that guide and reflexively nurture education's developmental mission. Learning aims and objectives are not pre-set according to an outcome-based preconception that valorises system-led initiatives (Kelly 2004). Instead, developmental goals are tied to what students do and the cultivated experiences during the learning process: the student is an active partner in his or her learning. The morphogenetic interplay between intersubjective proximity and its organisational background is guided by this reciprocal *symbolic code* of non-negation (the referential axis of the relation).

Relational Concepts and Practices

Organisational ties emerge from the *meta-reflexive* management of the interconnection between the referential and organisational axis. Whether individual or social, *meta-reflexive* management requires, in Freire's terms, 'critical consciousness' to engage in relations with the world (Freire 2000). Any learning intended to be educational develops the potential capacities of relationally autonomous learners and should change their direction in relation to the world (Freire in dialogue with Shor 1987a; Freire in dialogue with Shor 1987b). Participants are transformed when the concepts adopted and practices utilised are situated in and through their relationality with the world. So-called 'situated pedagogy'— explored in the next chapter — adapts learning, taking into account the shifting subjective access point at the beginning of each learning cycle.[6]

---

6 Subjective access points are identified in the socialised experiences of students; these experiences are an entry to critical investigation. Utilising access points, subject content is made relevant when approaching the object of investigation. Situated pedagogy is an implication of the two-way dialogue and part of the codification and de-codification process from which the content is re-presented to the students (see Chapter Six). While a subjective input point represents the developmental point of the student at the beginning of a learning cycle, subjective access points identify the

Subjective access points become the site of reciprocal exchanges between *Ego and Alter* that change the organisational dynamics and the diverse ways students are integrated into the learning process.

Furthermore, society is a network of networks, and the development of critical consciousness has ramifications for other social domains. In contrast to a system-based integration model, the critical consciousness developed in the relational model expands the horizons of value-patterns to cultural possibilities that transcend existing forms of mediation. Participants navigating the continuity between education and broader societal networks, buttressed by relational reciprocity, are encouraged and enabled to seek situated solutions within society's 'black box'.[7] Therefore, practices that change the learner's direction to the world are necessarily relationally referential and require solutions that are not extrinsically defined; they are directed instead by a relational theory of knowledge.

The Directive Liberating Approach

The development of learner autonomy does not mean the negation of interdependence between diverse levels of reality and the learner's place in the world. As argued, the person is emergent from natural, practical, and discursive orders and these orders work as both constraints and enablements. Learning and learner autonomy are inherently relational, as we cannot disengage from the world. Learners must co-create with teachers their autonomy — an idea that will be expanded in the next chapter; this model of relational education is not a *laissez-faire* approach to learning. Consequently, student ownership (enablement) of their learning is directed (constraint), leading to a 'directive liberating approach' — one that distinguishes the distinct roles of the teacher and student in learning relationships (Freire in dialogue with Shor 1987a; Freire in dialogue with Shor 1987b; Chambers 2019).

---

ongoing experiences of the students as part of the re-presentation of subject content within classroom dynamics.

7 The 'black box' refers to the internal dynamics of sociability — the social processes that generate transformation (morphogenesis) or reproduction (morphostasis) as an emergent relational effect.

In learning, the epistemic quadrangle is an evolutionary epistemology defined by the relational character of cognitive processes and how these processes are mediated between the observer and the world. The relational theory of knowing, however, does not mean an authoritarian regulation of freedom. Answers are not pre-given; instead, knowledge develops through open and critical mediation within relationships. The dialogical posture, according to Freire, is a direct response to epistemological inquietude as what is already known can be known better:

> In my view, each class is a class through which students and teachers engage in a search for the knowledge already obtained so they can adopt a dialogical posture as a response to their epistemological inquietude that forces the revision of what is already known so they can know it better (Freire in dialogue with Macedo 1995: 383).

As Freire suggests, in epistemological relationships, to direct the learner is to affirm the pre-existence of subject criteria and knowledge. Dialogue is a process of learning and knowing (Freire in dialogue with Macedo 1995), and the student is enabled to take part in this dialogue in line with pre-existing constraints of obtained knowledge (control). At the same time, the liberating aspect of this direction means the dialogical application of knowledge and learning cannot be disconnected from the learner's changing subjective access point. Thus, personal morphogenesis is still the referential component of practice. Based on the interplay of constraint and enablement, two realities should be considered:

1. Subject knowledge and criteria are embedded in an evolutionary cultural repository that mediates judgmental reason towards the object of reference. The importance of this knowledge is not negated when we start from the student's perspective.

2. The enablement of agentic authority means the learner is directed dialogically to utilise obtained knowledge when naming the object of knowledge. So, the goal is to develop the learner to use received mediations, then the learner becomes an object of knowledge for teachers. The teacher scaffolds the learner towards greater self-reliance and, in the process, situates existing mediations in reciprocal reference to the learner's morphogenesis. Therefore, mediations are not passively received but adapted to the learner's stage of development (the subjective access point). As each learner has an irreducible morphogenetic trajectory, then directing him or

her cannot become a disconnected judgement *of* learning. Instead, it collaborates with the learner *for* learning and is intrinsically tied to what the learner does as an active agent. A teacher, then, enables even as he or she constrains with direction, fostering relational participation and critical reflection in reference to the object of knowledge.

Concluding Remarks

This chapter aimed to show the implications of a relational epistemological approach for an alternative horizon that includes the level of face-to-face interactions and the formal patterns that organise these interactions. The chapter — continuing the theme of immanent critique — first looked to show the conceptual circularity of Parsons functionalist system-based AGIL scheme. In the functionalist scheme, social systems and their institutionalised relationships rely upon motivated individuals who can fulfil their status-roles. As the problem of integration is viewed as common to all types and modes of interactional orientation, value-orientations formulate what aspects of the cultural system are articulated as part of the motivation mechanisms of individual actors. The AGIL of the social system works parallel to the personality system with regard to the institutionalisation of value patterns that pre-exist in the bundle of status-roles. Therefore, the status-role becomes the essential concept in sociology and the fundamental category that integrates the personality system into the social system of interaction.

As is the case in the modernist *symbolic code*, the dyadic relationship between *Ego and Alter* is construed as something to be integrated into the pre-existing perspective of structured relationships. The AGIL scheme's relational turn as proposed in this chapter, however, views the autonomy of the learner — in the form of changing subjective access points — as something to be known rather than regulated. As a result, the AGIL scheme is rethought to put the transcendence of the human as the starting point (the value-horizon of the relation (L)). By placing the human element as the starting point, dyadic relationships from the perspective of Alter become the object of referential detachment that are managed *meta-reflexively* within the 'black box' of sociability. The morphogenetic relation between sociability and *relational goods* defines the mediations between both that enhance the value of the learner and learning.

The *ASV* produced in the educational process demonstrates the enrichment of sources of social capital through the reciprocal management of relations of proximity between *Ego and Alter*. The referential axis of AGIL views organisational ties (*religo*) through the prism of these relations of proximity. At the same time, relations of proximity are coordinated through the structural axis of AGIL. The structural axis directs the patterns of sociability in the *ASV* that renew relational goods. Hence, the synergy between *primary and secondary relational goods* ensures continuity between the referential and structural axis of AGIL. The shape of outcomes, in the form of formal settings, emerges in response to the referential axis and is based on the inner dynamics of learning. In terms of teaching and learning, three points are made salient:

1. Goals pursued are informed by reciprocal exchanges between interactants in reference to the relation's (L) dimension.

2. Relational concepts and practices are developed in situated ways that are responsive to the relational nature of cognitive processes.

3. The directive liberating approach means the development of the learner's autonomy is in relational dialogue with the world.

The dialectic between constraint and enablement implicates an understanding of subject criteria that pre-exists the learner and supplies avenues to revise the already known so it can be known better. Dialogue becomes a process that directs the learner in response to his changing subjective access points (the liberating dimension of enablement) when developing capabilities to know better. Within the interactive dynamics of teaching and learning, agentic authority is developed by scaffolding the learner towards greater self-reliance, considering subject knowledge and criteria. Thus, criteria are utilised in a responsive way to direct learning in dialogue with the learner's development.

6. Morphogenetic Education with a Developmental Mission

This chapter, expressing education's developmental mission, presents the continuity between different levels of sociability and the impact of this continuity on curriculum planning and assessment strategies. It affirms and expands two points:

1. Curriculum planning occurs in the context of a networked sociocultural ecology. By starting from relations of proximity, the design and application of learning from below means that the curriculum and assessment strategies adopted evaluate learning progress coherently from relations of proximity to all levels of this multi-dimensional ecology.

2. A curriculum that is co-created with the learner develops assessment strategies to document progress. The procedural mechanisms are designed to assist personal morphogenesis and not document achievement in reference to system-based status-roles. Adopting reflexive assessment practices within education's 'black box' also permits the system to adapt better to meet its developmental mission.

Curriculum Planning in the Context of a Networked Social Ecology

The reconstitutive process between sociability and *relational goods*, explored in previous chapters, is expanded in this section. It considers the idea of the curriculum as a *relational good* (a contextual resource) that produces ASV by regulating the interconnections between AGIL's referential and organisational axes. The idea is designed to meet students' developmental needs as a formalising contextual resource that organises teaching and learning. In terms of classroom practice, it stabilises the learning environment by providing direction and enabling active learning.

The contextual curriculum, as a primary *relational good*, is produced in partnerships and requires sovereign participants at stage T2–T3.[1] The resulting curriculum is an emergent contextual resource that is developed within schools and in relations between teachers, students, and administrators. Emerging from these primary relations and, as an outcome of *morphogenetic cycles*, it organises networked associations, which are characterised as secondary relations. The way the curriculum develops in the morphogenetic interplay between primary and secondary *relational goods* depends on the mediation of *Relational Subjects*. Curriculum development from below implies the primacy of de-centralised relations of proximity.

Contrary to system-led research, school-based research occurs in partnerships between sovereign participants. School-based research is an aspect of *relational reflexivity* that evaluates the delivered curriculum (a stabilising social mechanism) and its impact on learning progress (the referential aspect (L) of evaluation). The development of the delivered curriculum considers the conditions of sociability — the mode of production of *relational goods* — to be central to evaluations of the curriculum's efficacy as an evolving mechanism. In directing learning, its development is reciprocally tied to lived relations based on trust and cooperation. Therefore, evaluation and curriculum development are in reflexive dialogue through research responsive to the diverse properties that constitute teaching and learning (Kelly 2005). In planning the

---

[1] The curriculum as an adaptive, contextual resource is based on a three-fold distinction that operates relationally: the lived, planned (delivered), and experienced curriculum (Yancey 1998). The lived curriculum is the unique trajectory of learning at the start. Meanwhile, the planned curriculum outlines learning in syllabi, materials, and activities. The experienced curriculum denotes how the curriculum is planned and delivered in response to the learner's experiences. The nexus of these three strands — the lived, planned, and experienced curriculum — is the optimal place for learning (Yancey 1998:18). By taking the lived starting point — in the context of personal *morphogenetic cycles* — as the starting point, this model understands the experienced curriculum to affect the direction of the planned curriculum that optimises learning. Thus, contextually sensitive theories of practice are needed to maintain an alignment between the curriculum and the student's iteratively changing starting point (Yancey 1998: 8). As a primary *relational good*, situated pedagogy engages the student with the curriculum so that it is experienced (experienced curriculum) in ways that develop each starting point of a learning cycle (lived curriculum).

curriculum, there is harmony between its role as a secondary *relational good* and the concerns of those involved in making it a guide to enable teaching and learning.

The three-fold distinction of the curriculum — as lived, planned, and experienced — can be mapped to the different orders of social relationality (the processual or interactional and structural) (Donati 2021). At the processual or interactional stage (T2–T3), the curriculum is represented in its lived and experienced forms. The lived curriculum represents the starting point of the interactional stage of a learning cycle. The interactions that are responsive to the subjective access points of the learner are represented in the experienced curriculum. The relational order of structure is identified in the planned curriculum (stages T1 and T4) and is represented in pre-set and formalised syllabi. It guides teaching and learning at the beginning and emerges in a changed/reproduced social form in reflective adaptation to the teaching and learning dynamic in stage T2–T3. Below is an adapted diagram depicting Donati's different orders of social relationality. It illustrates this dynamic view of the curriculum as an organisational mechanism that binds and responds to the dynamics of teaching and learning relationships (Figure 8).

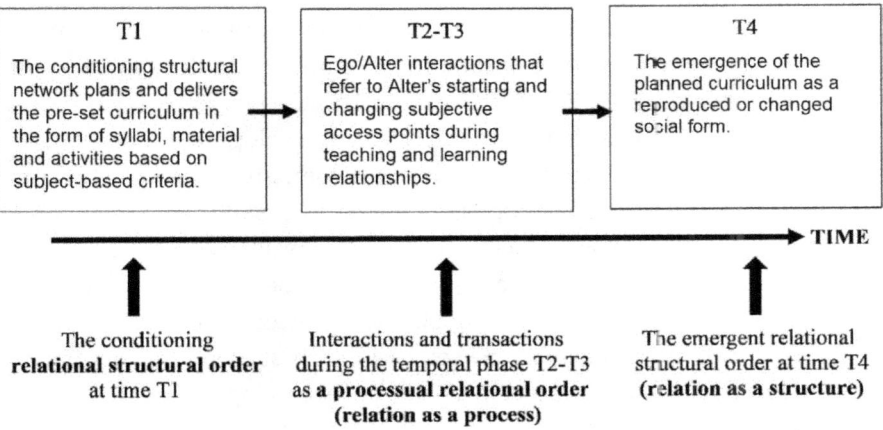

Fig. 8 The three-fold view of the curriculum as aspects of different orders of social relationality, adapted from Donati (2021: 56).

Planning Assessment to Buttress Learning

If assessment practice monitors and evaluates development, it becomes necessary to differentiate between *how* to assess and *what* to assess. The developmental question (the conceptual outcome) pertains to *what* to assess; however, *how* to assess (the outcome measure) is a strategic question regarding practices that best maximise the developmental principle (Astin and Antonio 2012). These two problems represent different facets of the AGIL compass — the conceptual outcome is the referential axis, and the outcome measure is the compass's organisational axis. In partnership with the student, what to assess will reference the subjective input point at the beginning of a learning cycle. The principle of development, when responsive to input points, frames assessment to bolster the learning process effectively. Such framing in developmental terms contrasts with system-based models that focus on outcomes before inputs.

Assessment strategies that attend to the referential axis are organised to evaluate learning in ways that put talent development first. The method discounts norm-referenced assessment because it is a model that is not focused on the internal dynamics of learning but seeks instead to measure outcomes to a performance curve without recourse to the learner's input point. Outcome measures disconnected from input points, in the form of one-off summative grades, do not offer insight into whether progress has occurred and what needs to be done inside the 'black box' of learning to scaffold learner development. Competitive assessment regimes that inherently seek to compare and select students are designed not to develop students but to sanction and restrict 'excellence' through an artificial credentialing process.

To re-discover the human-in-the-social, the educational aim is to develop *all* students. Learning should be evaluated in reference to the personal morphogenetic trajectory of each student and organised in ways that do not restrict progress in achieving learning criteria. Assessments that buttress development, therefore, are both criterion-referenced and self-referential. They are criterion-referenced in that they acknowledge inherited knowledge mediations; they are self-referential insofar as they do not restrict any learner from progressing to achieve these outcomes. This way, learners are not compared to each other, and all, potentially, can achieve subject criteria based on individual learning plans. By contrast, the system-based mode of governance encourages the assessment *of* learning because its focus is to judge and select the right students that meet role expectations.

In the system-based model, the priority given to credentialing in a competitive assessment regime means institutions operate on the premise of sanctioned 'excellence' that treats students as a potential resource. Institutions therefore compete to enhance prestige and reputation by producing optimal assessment outcomes or selecting the 'best' students based on previous assessment outcomes (through selection, the aim is to produce optimal future outcomes). Based on a zero-sum competition, the 'reputation and prestige' institutional model is outcome-focused, that is, it aims to own artificially restricted 'excellence' as a resource to further its reputation and thereby access further resources.

When development is the mission of education, then an alternative system framework can be articulated — one that does not operate from an insular institutional logic of 'reputation and prestige' (Astin and Antonio 2012: 275). In this diverging framework, the climate is one of 'institutional transcendence' , that is, it is defined as one in which 'excellence' is something that transcends what institutions do to enhance themselves. 'Excellence' is defined instead by relations that reference *all* students and start from individual input points to develop progress authentically. The absence of artificial selectivity means excellence is open to *all* in articulations of sociability defined by reciprocity at the inter-institutional level. Formulating this institutional transcendence, Astin and Antonio (2012) propose a cooperative system perspective in which institutions work together and contribute to one mission: talent development. Together, institutions contribute to social value by pooling resources, research, and innovative practices that effectively bridge the divide between student entry-point and sought outcomes:

> When we operate from the narrow perspective of one institution or a single profession, we are concerned only with what happens to those students we admit; the rejected candidates are not of interest to us. On the other hand, when we view such decision problems from a larger system perspective, we concern ourselves with the fate of all candidates, winners and rejects alike (Astin and Antonio 2012: 226).

The Interplay between Learner Agency and Learning Criteria

External to the student's subjective input point is the pre-existence of learning criteria. As standards of excellence do not operate in a logic of achievement — to credential some learners — the learning criteria become part of the coordination and co-production of teaching and learning relationships. Two points are raised to affirm learner agency in this logic of coordination and co-creation:

1. The understanding of emergent personhood discussed in previous chapters implicates an 'in-gear' conception of freedom (Collier 1994). This means that the student's relative autonomy is always relational to the natural, practical, and discursive worlds.

2. Combining an 'in-gear' understanding of learning and returning with Freire's notion of the directive liberating approach, the teacher and student both have different roles in a problem-posing dialogical model.

Regarding the first point, an 'in-gear' conception of freedom follows an evolutionary and referential view of knowledge generation. It describes an understanding that the person develops through his or her interactions with the world. We are not free to choose, Collier argues, while disengaged from the world:

> This metaphor, I hope, is clear enough: in-gear freedom is a matter of interacting causally with the world in order to realise our intentions; it is threatened by any view which denies the efficacy of our intentions in bringing about changes in the real world; out-of-gear freedom is precisely a matter of disengaging our choices from causal interaction with the world, to ward off the threat that the nature of that world might limit or determine them. One instance of an out-of-gear conception of freedom is expressed by Rorty [in *Philosophy and the Mirror of Nature* (1979)]: 'Man is always free to choose new descriptions (for, among other things, himself)' (Collier 1994: 98).

Student autonomy (that is, understanding and judgement) develops within interactions. These interactions occur in a pre-existing world, and inherited knowledge content is necessarily emergent from interactions in this world. At the same time, interaction is mediated and contested; therefore, students are encouraged to develop critical capacities through a problem-posing dialogical pedagogy. Dialogue, according to Freire, represents an epistemological relationship in which the development of critical capacities is tied to its social relationality:

> I engage in dialogue because I recognise the social and not merely the individualistic character of the process of knowing. In this sense, dialogue presents itself as an indispensable component of the process of both learning and knowing (Freire in dialogue with Macedo 1995: 379).

Moving on to the second point, the object of dialogue is built on the student's experiences while directing these experiences utilising the necessary tools and skills to apprehend the cognisable object of knowledge. Accordingly, two interrelated strands of Freire's directive liberating approach are brought together: the first strand is the directive role of the teacher that distinguishes between the responsibilities of teacher and student; the second affirms the importance of the student's starting point and the experiences brought into the learning process. The difference between directive and authoritarian education is that the former acknowledges the interchange between teacher and student in which both co-create the plan of learning and knowing; the latter is a top-down imposition that takes no account of student variation. Between these two strands, there is an interplay (co-direction) in which the teacher's authority directs learning but in a dialogical way. The liberating teacher uses authority within the limits of freedom (enabling learner agency) with students as co-directors of the curriculum (Freire in dialogue with Shor 1987a: 91).

In contrast to transmission models of learning and knowing, authority emerges from the relation itself and is not imposed on the student. Directive authority (control) is adaptable because it responds to the needs of students and their learning. The student must be directed to overcome naïve and common-sense assumptions to enable referential detachment and, thus, critical exchange with the object. In the second strand noted above — the freedom of the learner to co-create both learning and knowing — dialogue becomes essential to generate partnership in the moment of 'communication between the cognitive subjects, the subjects who know, and who try to know' (Freire in dialogue with Shor 1987a: 99).

Freedom implies an activated learner who participates in creating outcomes based on their developmental situation. Freire's directive liberating approach thus connects dialogic inquiry to situated pedagogy: the teacher recognises the learner's subjective entry point at the beginning of a learning cycle. Pedagogy becomes situated in as much as it continuously seeks to present and represent the required material, considering the student's comprehension of daily experiences and how they relate to the object. In the descriptions of everyday life, subjective limits become access points for the teacher to enable a rigorous and critical understanding of reality (Freire in dialogue with Shor 1987: 106). The curriculum, therefore, is a script that continuously changes based on the dynamics of the situation, that is, the subjective trajectory of the student as they try to know in new ways.

The situated dimension of the teacher's directive role also requires the framing of the teacher's authority in reference to what students do. It seeks to cultivate self-directed learners whose critical exchanges with others are the *raison d'etre* for transmitted knowledge that builds rigorously formed explanations. The teacher, in this process, is an artist who re-invents classroom practices and assessment strategies, considering the required competencies that underpin development. Planning of the curriculum's script is mapped to developing access points located inside the learning situation. The teacher makes the subject relevant to the student through the initial 'codification' of lived situations (the experienced curriculum) that are decodified as part of a prolonged critical investigation (Freire in dialogue with Shor 1987a: 115).[2]

Directive liberating education, in orchestrating prolonged critical investigations, encourages in-gear engagement with and changes in the real world. It is directed by the authority of knowledge (Collier 1994: 98) to facilitate studies grounded in everyday interactions in the world. Accordingly, the unsettling of received 'codifications' constitutes

---

2   Codification starts from the situation of the learner in the world. The teacher collaborates with students to create codifications of experiences from being in the world with others (these codifications are representations that can take different forms). According to Freire, 'generative themes' can be decoded from the original codifications created in co-investigation between the teacher and students. The critical investigation results in the recodification of the original codifications as part of a prolonged study (Freire 2000; Burstow 1991). When subject knowledge is connected to subjective access points, it gains relevance to the students' lived situations that are decodified into themes, utilising subject-based criteria as students mature to learn in new ways.

the *Relational Subjects* that transform existing relationships between students, teachers, schools, and society (Freire in dialogue with Shor 1987b). Collaborative relationships between students and teachers are part of a broader process in which the role expectations of both sets of agents are rethought and sealed in dialogue.

The Synergy between Criterion-Referenced Assessment and Ipsative Assessment

The previous section discussed the interplay between learner agency and the directive role of learning criteria. In this section, I seek to apply the implications of this interplay to an alternative assessment model that synergises criterion-referenced and ipsative assessment.[3] This synergy aims to incorporate learning criteria inside the learning dynamics as it operates as a directive guide.[4] Bearing in mind Freire's directive liberating education, the synergy involves the cooperation of teacher and student in planning learning goals. The partnership monitors learning progress — the ipsative dimension of assessment — and defines *which* outcomes are assessed (the referential axis of AGIL). The criteria provide guiding milestones on the *how* of assessment. Two points distinguish the synergy between criterion-referenced assessment and ipsative assessment:

1. Ipsative assessment is the value reference when evaluating learning. Criterion-referenced assessment can be coupled with norm-referenced or ipsative assessment. In the norm-referencing case, the goal of assessment is to promote the values of competition and selection in which learners are graded and categorised for credentialing. In the ipsative case, learning excellence is not relative to other students; instead, as will be clarified, the goal is for students to meet and creatively engage with learning criteria. How

---

[3] Ipsative assessment is a learner-referenced development model that evaluates learning by comparing existing performance to previous performance (Hughes 2014).

[4] Again, the system-based competitive assessment regime, de-focusing input points, is inherently designed to exclude some learners by utilising learning criteria as a measuring stick to categorise based on grade bands. As stated before, this approach, based on an ethos of achievement, is selective and does not seek to develop learners inclusively.

criterion-referenced assessment is used cannot be separated from the value reference of both learning and knowing.

2. Recognising student entry points upholds the human-in-the-social. The ipsative assessment model stresses the dynamics underpinning learning progress. These dynamics are environmental factors that guide students to become self-regulated learners capable of self-directed learning. As ipsative assessment is self-referential, *all* students can meet the learning criteria. The learning environment enables students to bridge learning gaps to meet the learning criteria determined by their different entry points (Astin and Antonio 2012). Thus, acknowledging inclusivity, the human factor always comes first when evaluating learning.

In learner growth, the authority of assessment criteria is in tension with liberty. However, from this tension (constraint), student freedoms can emerge (enablement). According to Freire, growth and maturity — part of personal *morphogenetic cycles* — are the effects of the self-discipline that develops between authority and freedom:

> Dialogue means a permanent tension in the relation between authority and liberty. But, in this tension, authority continues to be because it has authority vis-à-vis permitting students freedoms which emerge, which grow and mature, precisely because authority and freedom learn self-discipline (Freire in dialogue with Shor 1987a: 102).

The authority of standards, this way, is identified in learning criteria that are woven into the fabric of learning. They exist as milestones and a long-term compass for the non-linear development of self-directed learning. Consequently, criterion-referenced assessment is compatible with an ipsative logic of progress. Criteria are not something to be attained but are a license from below to enable students the freedom to overcome a naïve understanding of the world and their place in it. When criteria are personalised, the performance is not defined in reference to standardisation and a competitive grading system.[5] Standards are no

---

5 There is a difference between performance standards and externally set standardisation of learning outcomes. The curriculum is narrowed in an externally set standardisation of learning outcomes, and learners are set targets to achieve. Regardless of the learner's starting point, he or she is graded according to a pre-existing and externally set standard. Criterion-referenced assessment does not have to be imposed from above; instead, *how* it is designed and enacted is key to making it compatible with progress-driven assessment.

longer assigned universally to groups and instead relate to the student's work and awareness of assessment criteria that guide that work.

A Network of Reflective Institutions that Document Learning

The emphasis on subjective developmental points has practical implications at the level of inter-institutional cooperation. As discussed above, institutional transcendence entails a developmental mission that replaces the 'prestige and reputation' approach existing in education (an ethos that seeks to exploit rather than develop talent (Astin and Antonio 2012)). If the long-term goal is to build self-reliance in learning, it is necessary to continuously document key entry points and exit points in each learning cycle. This documentation informs and is informed by school-based research, acting as a repository of practices that effectively bridge these two points to buttress personal growth. The focus on changing developmental points implicates an assessment regime whose responsive practices scaffold the learner towards freedom through the self-disciplined continuous mastery of the underlying *raison d'etre* of the object studied. Inter-institutional cooperation at the system level entails reflectivity and adaptation in response to the efficacy of practices in making this scaffolding effective. The documentation of entry and exit points is accompanied by further documentation of what occurs within the noted interplay between authority and liberty to produce personal development from one to the other.

In order to sustain self-disciplined learning, it becomes vital that institutions share a longitudinal cross-institutional database that documents the student's perspective within learning cycles (Astin and Antonio 2012). Documentation of the student's perspective ensures that the learning process is planned coherently and does not miss vital developmental stages. Specifically, such a database allows visibility of the student's grasp of underlying criteria of critical investigations prior to the start of each learning cycle. The incorporation of criterion-referenced assessment into classroom learning provides milestone guidelines and a reference point for the documentation of progress. Documenting individual learning also ensures that resources can be deployed to impact progress in coordination between institutions.

Reflective institutions are part of broader societal governance in which there is interdependence between *primary, secondary, and generalised forms of sociability* to produce *relational goods* at every level. As part of relational societal governance, the dynamic between personal, collective, and social reflexivity results in a repository of research-based strategies that potentially transform teaching and learning. The outcome of this reflexive process is a reflective inter-institutional system perspective whose interconnected networks coordinate to develop talent and contribute to expanding the parameters of sociability. An inter-institutional database of learning documentation enables each student to participate actively in the planning of their education, regardless of their distinctive input points. The following section focuses on strategies at the *primary level of sociability* and the different ways situated assessment practices can be incorporated into classroom relations to stimulate learning in a coherent and connected way.

Structured Learning through Mentorship

Learning is multi-dimensional and non-linear.[6] As such, it requires a curriculum that provides structure to education but does not use criteria to measure this learning. The non-linear nature of development means that learning involves an inventiveness by which students are expected to arrive at solutions from the fundamental principles of investigation. Cultivating an ethic of discovery — the underlying *raison d'etre* of the object studied — enables a capacity to be aware of monitoring and self-evaluating progress (learning *how* to learn). The idea of learning criteria that guides developmental milestones requires long-term mentoring. Mentors act in relationships to support students to reflect on how they think as, for example, sociologists. Mentorship is a directed invitation to students to explore the inner craft of the intellect embedded in the context of a 'relationship-based cognitive apprenticeship' (Gleibermann, n.d.: 4).

---

6   Non-linear learning criteria are understood and applied differently by individual learners (situated pedagogy). Starting from the student's perspective implicates the planning of learning in ways that are artistically applied in the classroom within teaching and learning partnerships.

Such an apprenticeship develops the reflective capacity of the mentee in a structured and systematic way. To be self-aware of the cognitive processes of learning means starting from the fundamental epistemological foundations that form the basis for building tools and strategies to approach the object of experience (Worley 2018). For example, the relational approach is the epistemic framework through which the *morphogenetic paradigm* is developed; the application of its methodological strategies and tools is guided by the epistemological conditions of sociology as a knowledge system. Without having been inculcated into a systematic way of thinking, the learner cannot provide justified explanations on adopting strategies and how they were utilised in the process of thinking.

A coherent learning plan should start by mentoring meta-cognitive skills in the shape of learning criteria that provide the foundation of the student's cognitive apprenticeship. The goal is to develop his or her capacity to regulate and understand internal cognitive processes in ways that nurture independent and active learning. Again, as Freire argues, there can be no autonomy without concomitant direction that develops in relationships. The enablement of students' freedom emerges from these relationships, but students need first to be directed or constrained to develop the inner craft to utilise this freedom. Only then will they become aware of what constitutes progress as learners. The inner craft that explains the object, in communication with others, stresses the structure of the subject (Bruner 1999).

The Ipsative Dimension of Structured Learning

Structured learning that references the relationship between the learner and his world is necessarily emergent from relationship-based interactions. The focus on input points — the subjective organisation and re-organisation of experiences — means that the goals of structured learning shift in line with a learner's progress. The re-organisation of experiences is an active and reflective act based on interactions with the environment. Thus, education is embedded in the dialectic between oneself and the world — the dialectic has implications for both the student and the world that generates experiences. The dialectic also means continuity with the daily life experiences of learners (an 'in-gear' view of learning in the world).

When education starts with the student, mechanisms intended to bring about pre-set learning outcomes become inadequate. They cannot sustain learning beyond one-off summative assessments and the underlying pedagogy of teaching to these outcomes. Without concern for interaction, learning becomes disconnected at the personal level and develops into random criteria without a coherent interconnectedness between its different elements. Outcomes designed without regard for input points and interactions lead to a passive and sterile education disconnected from the learner and his or her world (Rodgers 2002: 847).

A student's experiences offer situated access points in the context of long-term development, that is, the organisation and re-organisation of subjective experiences. These access points provide relevant themes that teachers can use creatively. The responsive nature of situated pedagogy means teaching becomes an artistic process that utilises changing access points to continuously re-represent the material. In response to the learner's perspective — the ipsative dimension of assessment — learning outcomes are evaluated and revised according to progress. The goals evaluated at an outcome point are ipsative when they are progress-defined in reference to the individual student (Hughes 2014). Student participation, therefore, is tied to the subjective experiences they bring into learning. Directive liberating education is authentic insofar as it makes use of development points that license the learner to develop within progress-defined and criterion-referenced learning outcomes. The artistic teacher does not deliver learning; instead, he or she mentors active students into new perceptions and creative learning. Taking account of the subjective input points of each student redraws the curriculum and its learning outcomes in partnership with teachers and administrators.

Structured Learning Requires the Formation of Assessment Literacy

The idea of structured learning that is self-referential in its design and application highlights the importance of developing assessment literacy to connect these two dimensions. Assessment operates at two interconnected levels (Hughes 2014):

1. The student's awareness of assessment criteria.
2. The evaluation of work produced considers meta-level subject skills found in the assessment's aims and criteria.

Specifically, the development of meta-cognitive capacities is fundamental to the self-reliant student who understands what constitutes progress and how to sustain this progress. Practices that promote talent development, therefore, should incorporate assessment literacy into the dialogics of classroom activities. The student's perspective to self-regulate learning is continuously observed, reviewed, and renewed in morphogenetic growth cycles. Incorporating assessment practices into learning means its design and application constantly seek to further learning in the systematic and coherent way described above. An assessment regime that seeks self-aware learning will scaffold the student towards greater self-reliance. The student's growing literacy to evaluate progress constitutes deep learning and promotes greater autonomy. Through this coherent approach, teacher dependency can be curtailed, and the learner becomes an active participant in setting his or her own goals. Again, criteria effectively enter the work produced when the student appreciates how these criteria guide their progress. The instrumentalism of pre-set learning outcomes, disconnected from the learner, promotes dependency through disjointed learning — the learner is rendered passive when assessment universally judges a cohort and does not guide personalised learning.

Mentoring the student to reason from fundamental principles ensures a structured direction sustained through an awareness of deep systematic learning. The integration of this two-level approach to assessment also means a learner-directed curriculum. According to Hughes, the aims and objectives of a learner-directed curriculum should be aligned with assessment practices that respond to the changing starting points of the student. As assessment literacy grows, the learner is then capable of connecting the curriculum's pre-set requirements to personal goals and interests:

> Assessment should be deliberately or constructively aligned with curriculum aims and objectives. This avoids mismatch between learner

position and aims/objectives. In a learner directed curriculum the learner undertakes projects and activities with pre-set requirements but have scope for learners to set their own goals according to interests and starting points (Hughes 2014: 48).

Incorporating Assessment Literacy into Assessment Practices

Developed in partnership with the student, the teacher's incorporation of assessment literacy into assessment practices is a *meta-reflexive* activity. The goal, as stated above, is to maintain harmony between the learner's position and the curriculum's aims and objectives (the criteria that guide development). Assessment is intrinsic to learning cycles and is bound to personal morphogenesis to ensure long-term harmony. It is thus embedded in each stage of the process — at the beginning, stage T2–T3 and, finally, when evaluating outcomes. Pre-assessment, therefore, provides an avenue to ascertain past experiences and a perspective on how they may shape future changes.

As post-assessment reflection is retrospective, it can be incorporated simultaneously into formative pre-assessment when it looks forward to the next cycle. The reflective movement from past to current experience is central to a personal morphogenetic reorganisation of experience. It encourages referential detachment (the foundation of meta-cognitive skills), establishing cognitive distance through the internalisation of learning criteria as meaningful milestones integral to directing learning progress. Putting assessment literacy at the centre of assessment activities requires qualitative forms of assessment that can evaluate deep learning that includes *cognitive and affective outcomes*. These different forms of learning are interconnected and are not reducible to one-size-fits-all standardisation.

In the mentoring process, self- and peer-review activities can be used to differentiate rather than standardise learners. Actuating practices that focus on assessment literacy means giving students a voice in evaluating their work and the work of others; this empowerment is an essential factor in motivating long-term learning (Hughes 2014). It allows the student to think about how he or she is thinking and to apply these skills in the completion and evaluation of his or her work. The enablement of activities that enhance assessment literacy can be incorporated into and change the nature of assignments (Tanner 2012). Promoting self-evaluation changes the focus of assignments towards a teacher-directed ipsative assessment approach.

Activities that connect criterion-referenced and ipsative assessment vis-à-vis assessment literacy through applying criteria are necessarily reflexive. Below are examples of ipsative-based activities that show strategies that potentially promote this reflexivity and can be incorporated into assignments:

1. Keeping reflective journals: Reflective journals or diaries, monitored by teachers, allow students to write down their thoughts on *how* assessment criteria were used to produce assignments. A journal is a flexible self-review strategy that can be incorporated into assignments. It encourages students to document explicitly how the meanings ascribed to their experiences are transformed through relationships and interactions formed in their learning environment (Tanner 2012). Students' reflections on *how* they are learning also plays an essential role in adapting the curriculum to align with their progress. For example, teachers can modify the curriculum and teaching direction by identifying points of confusion.

2. Demonstrating long-term development through work portfolios: Maintaining a documented archive of assignments is an essential strategy in ipsative assessment. The long-term work portfolio is intrinsically connected to changing starting points in personal morphogenesis. The inclusion of reflective journals within portfolios also adds a meta-cognitive dimension to the documentation of work produced. Documentation of long-term learning strengthens a dynamic curriculum and responsive teaching

3. Peer-reviewed activities: Different strategies can encourage students to share evaluations. For example, teachers can mentor students to emulate the teacher's role as facilitator. In this role, the student demonstrates an awareness of the evaluation criteria by interacting and prompting learning direction with other students (Worley 2018). Such acts of facilitation produce reflective partnerships and incorporate assessment strategies into classroom practice. Working collaboratively, students systematically evaluate their learning, for example, by encouraging each other to make their pre-suppositions explicit in order to show deep and systematic learning (Yancey 1998). Students led to think about their thinking in this way may

then demonstrate how the learning criteria guide their learning actively and coherently.

4. Connecting learning between course modules: Deep learning is systematic and starts from a meta-cognitive reflection on *how* to think within a subject. For example, there is a continuous need to make general pre-suppositions explicit when adopting an analytical framework, research methods, and techniques in sociology. Without clear connections between theoretical and empirical modules, learning becomes disjointed. Nurturing assessment literacy through reflection, however, builds awareness of how underlying criteria — the basis of assessment literacy — produces analytical interconnections within and between disciplines.

Based on the identification of subjective access points, the contextually sensitive approach to assessment maintains learning continuity and builds on the changing experiences of the learner. It emerges from interactive relationships that instil an ethic of discovery. The student is inculcated with habits that enable him or her to witness their learning (Yancey 1998). Feedback is focused on developing learner agency and the ability of students to demonstrate *how* they are learning and producing works. The interactive dynamic is oriented toward developing active learners that learn coherently and interactively:

> As they learn, they witness their own learning: they show us how they learn. Reflection makes possible a new kind of learning as well as a new kind of teaching. The portraits of learning that emerge here point to a new kind of classroom: one that is coherently theorised, interactive, oriented to agency (Yancey 1998: 8).

Instead of grade bands, long-term cognitive, affective, and behavioural changes mark progress and are recorded in a cross-institutional database. The teacher employs this database to align assessment strategy and feedback to the learner's changing starting point.

The coherent planning of learning according to subjective developmental points ensures student agency is acknowledged. When the assessment is also oriented towards a student's agency, his or her long-term self-directed development becomes possible through a meta-cognitive realisation (self-awareness) of how he or she changes as a learner (the lived curriculum). This realisation entails being reflective through retrospectively examining experiences and what was done in each assignment to fulfil the learning criteria (Tanner 2012).

Concluding Remarks

In this chapter, I built on the idea of a relational continuity between different organisational levels of sociability (the structural axis of AGIL). Mapping the educational context onto the referential axis of AGIL, I proposed the need to acknowledge continuity in the development of the self-reliant learner and *Relational Subject*. The planning and delivery of the curriculum were presented as a strategy to organise learning based on how the student experiences it. As a contextual resource, the curriculum is both a *primary and secondary relational good* as part of a networked. Bearing in mind the stratified reality of a networked reality, a three-fold distinction of the curriculum was posited — the lived, delivered, and experienced curriculum. The delivered curriculum acknowledges relationships of proximity and adapts in response to them; in its lived and experienced form (a primary *relational good*), the curriculum is guided by its delivered format.

For curriculum to document learning development in reference to the lived experiences of the student, the planning of teaching and learning needs adaptive mechanisms that reflexively respond to its internal dynamics (the 'black box' of sociability) to produce *ASV*. Within the 'black box', the lived curriculum — as a primary relation good — connects the interactive dynamics at stage T2–T3 with its morphogenetic outcomes. The result is a license from below to make use of de-centralised relations of proximity so as to guide the emergent features of the curriculum as a stabilising mechanism (delivered curriculum) within processes of sociability.

If the delivered curriculum guides and provides the learning outlines, assessment monitors and evaluates development. Two assessment dimensions need to be distinguished — the procedural dimension looks at *how* to assess outcomes, and the conceptual pertains to *what* to assess. First, the procedural dimension is an adaptive strategy designed to maximise learning development. The conceptual dimension, meanwhile, is tied to the student's changing input points in each morphogenetic learning cycle. Strategies are designed using to monitor and document learning. This documentation provides pathways within the 'black box' that enable the adaptation of practices to ensure they effectively scaffold the learner towards greater self-reliance.

In system-based modes of assessment, the curriculum is pre-given, and externally determined standards are imposed on students regardless of their input point. Such competitive assessment aims to exploit talent — based on distinguishing standardised performance levels and identifying 'excellence' — rather than to develop capabilities. This model, in seeking to credential learners for pre-given status-roles, sets students up to fail. When standards are incorporated into the personal development process, however, they do not artificially restrict the achievement of outcomes. On a system level, institutions can further the mission of talent development. They do this by coordinating their activities to produce *ASV* through pooling resources, research, and innovation that effectively bridge the divide between the learner's entry-point and exit point in each personal *morphogenetic cycle*.

An 'in-gear' view of the emergence of subjective access points means the path between entry-point and exit-point requires attention to the constraints in the natural, practical, and discursive orders. Personal maturity and growth must be directed considering prior 'codifications' of investigated objects. Hence, due to the interplay between learning standards, the directive liberating approach is a situated pedagogy that understands the authority and direction of criteria to be enacted within the dialogic inquiry. Adapting to the student's experiences — represented in his or her changing access points — entails a view of the curriculum as a script that varies based on collaborative dynamics that enable students to know in new ways.

Furthermore, an in-gear and relationship-based view of learning recognises personal reflexivity in its relationality to the natural, practice, and discursive realities that generate the object of critical investigation. As learning is to be evaluated in reference to the epistemic relations generated from these realities, the pre-existing criteria that emerge from these relations should be woven into teaching and learning. Integration of criterion-referenced assessment into the learner's development implicates an interaction with ipsative assessment and the documentation of personal growth in reference to the authority of received mediations. Consequently, the directive role in educational partnerships monitors learning progress in a non-linear way (the ipsative dimension) to ascertain *which* outcomes are assessed (AGIL's referential axis).

The authority and directive role of criteria, enacted within formative assessment activities, enables self-discipline. In turn, self-discipline underpins the capability to self-monitor development and evaluate progress in a self-referenced way. Nurturing the inner craft of the subject within relationship-based cognitive apprenticeships leads to a coherent and structured learning environment that connects subject knowledge to the meta-cognitive skills needed to undertake projects and activities. When pedagogy is situated and responsive to learners' access points, education is a verb in which activated students orchestrate their own study. Self-awareness of assessment literacy promotes and is part of developing deep learning and self-reliance. Moreover, promoting deep learning and greater autonomy harmonises the learner's position with the curriculum's aims and objectives, setting the direction of learning partnerships. The reflexive skills needed for referential detachment — the starting point of critical investigation — are milestones integral to the aims and objectives of the learning process.

Connecting the curriculum to evaluation requires forms of assessment activity that allow for the demonstration of deep learning. This chapter proposed different activities that align criteria-referenced and ipsative-referenced forms of assessment. In the context of structured and deep learning, a focus on assessment literacy is presented to align both assessment forms. Activities such as keeping reflective journals, peer-reviewed undertakings, and connecting learning between course modules are attempts to sustain joined-up and integrated learning. Thus, changes in *cognitive outcomes* — subject knowledge and its criteria — generate *affective outcomes* (self-reliance and self-discipline). When standards are self-referenced, the student, in active partnership, demonstrates agency in how they are learning (the referential axis of AGIL).

7. A Summary of the Argument Presented

In this final chapter, I will summarise the argument presented in this book. Below is an outline of the argument, followed by further exposition of each point:

1. In hegemonic approaches to policy, the functionalist conceptual infrastructure is incapable of acknowledging the human element in policy initiatives and practices. Instead of managing differentiation relationally, the system-based perspective defines the parameters of knowledge. Thus, the state intervenes to ensure interactive dynamics enable individuals to meet system needs.

2. Aware that such governance models are epistemically closed, an alternative general framework is needed to guide the logic of social policies and interventions.

3. Based on a relational realism, the *morphogenetic paradigm* explains the co-emergence of the human and social. If policies reference the *latent ontological reality* of the human-in-the-social, it is first necessary to explain personal morphogenesis.

4. To enter the dynamics of social relations is to emphasise the role of social reflexivity in the process of social capitalisation. The concept of social capital is understood in a disentangled way to include the temporal stages and elements of morphogenetic processes.

5. A relational realist application of Parsons's AGIL scheme is proposed. The scheme provides a compass to articulate contextually sensitive practices whose properties are reflexivity transformed in response to the latent dimension of social relations (the human person).

6. A contextually sensitive model of teaching and learning is expressed in the interplay between direction and liberation. The organisational

and structural aspect of AGIL is devised as a networked ecology that is reflexively responsive to relations of proximity.

System-Based *Lib/Lab* Triangulation

Based on modernity's *symbolic code*, the conceptual make-up of UK *lib/lab* governance models negate the human element. The referential dimension of these different models is expressed in initiatives that aim to regulate the exchange parameters between *Ego and Alter* (to reproduce an economically productive social order). Alter's role is articulated between the individual and collective (*homo economicus* and *homo sociologicus*) in which the self-maximising individual operates in state-regulated environments that provide opportunities (public goods). As public goods are attached to status-roles, participants are not sovereign in making them. Opportunities, according to the logic of fairness, are provided to enable *homo economicus* to operate within a situational logic of competition within a self-professed meritocratic regime.

From New Labour to Conservative approaches, different models espouse the discourse of devolution and the need to transcend inadequate rigid ideological templates. However, in practice, we have an existing state-defined mission that appropriates the processes of sociability and the parameters of knowable reality. When devolution is proposed, the acts of reference — values, rules, and contextual resources — are conceptualised from a state-based perspective. What is possible, in an epistemic sense, is inherently limited in its possibilities.

A Model of Governance based on the Relational Realist Approach

Due to the limitations of modernity's *symbolic code* and its accompanying functionalist *symbolic reference*, an alternative is needed to explain the emergence of the human-in-the-social. A *philosophical ontology*, relational realism is based on a meta-theoretical approach that starts from the epistemic dynamics between the act of reference and referent. The referential detachment between *Ego and Alter*, mediated in its socio-cultural context, is the basis of transcendental realism. Because knowledge is derived from the conditions of its emergence, the relational approach advocated is a transcendental realism that does not dictate epistemic parameters in a pre-defined way. Instead, relational realism views the possibilities of knowledge within relations of proximity and the wider place of their emergence (the site of their emergence includes the broader contingencies of a networked social reality).

As the constitution of Alter is irreducible to the contingencies of relations, epistemic relativity leads to *judgemental rationality*. Thus, to explain the emergence of Alter, equally relational referential acts are needed that include existing socio-cultural mediations. When the relationship is the first ontological premise, the conditions of emergence become central to an understanding of the object of reference. The *morphogenetic paradigm* is a paradigm that explains the emergence of Alter from within the interplay of agent-subjects and socio-cultural structures.

Judgemental rationality is enacted by adopting the *morphogenetic paradigm* and utilising methodological research tools and research-based policies and practices guided by this paradigm. The research outcomes of *judgemental rationality* produce theories that reflect a relational understanding of social reality. Thus, the objective of a relational realist approach is to develop a conceptual paradigm and tools that explain the distinction between the human and the social. From this distinction, an alternative policy blueprint can be established that acknowledges the emergence of the human-in-the-social as the referential axis of governance.

The basis of this alternative blueprint is the epistemic quadrangle. It specifies a scheme for analysing interchanges within relations. In this quadrangle, the first triangle refers to the observer and the second one to the *latent ontological reality* of the perceived object. The relation between the upper and lower triangle is mediated by existing referential acts (socio-cultural mediations) the parameters of which reference the *latent reality* of the object in the lower triangle (the development of potential powers). As the referent in the lower triangle emerges from these mediations between the upper and lower triangles, there is a crucial role played by the *judgemental rationality* of agent-subjects — as *Relational Subjects* — in normalising the ontology of the lower triangle. The normalisation of the referent through the transformation of existing mediations is a morphogenetic process that includes relations of proximity to broader stabilising mechanisms in the form of socio-cultural structures.

The Morphogenetic Paradigm and Personhood

Socio-cultural mediations between the upper and lower triangle give rise to the person. The *morphogenetic paradigm* accounts for the emergence of personal identity from these mediations. If social interventions answer the normative question in a transcendental way, then an account needs to be provided of the past, present, and future trajectories of personal and socio-cultural morphogenesis. The normative question is approached through the *meta-reflexive* activity of *Relational Subjects* who acknowledge the trajectory of personal morphogenesis (personal morphogenesis being the ground of relating to Alter). In the case of education, for example, student development is based on assessment activities that are responsive to changing starting points in morphogenetic learning cycles.

The *morphogenetic paradigm* investigates how personal identity develops in a world-directed interplay between personal deliberations and the context of these deliberations. The relationality between the human and the social implicates an explanation of how the indexical 'I' is individually sensed as a socially indexed device, that is, how the indexical 'I' reaches an alignment between itself and a pre-existing third-person social identity. In this alignment process, the role requirements of the social identity generate concerns that are reflexively navigated. The subjective authority regarding third-person reality is presupposed by a capability to deliberate on this reality. This deliberation leads to the individual dedicating himself to a role and its behavioural outcomes.

As deliberation encompasses the full spectrum of reality, subjective engagement is pre-dependent on the practical order from which reflexive human properties and powers emerge. These properties and powers sustain the sense of self and the propositional elaborations in reference to the discursive world. As a result, the distinction between molecules and meanings is necessary logically and in an explanatory sense when explaining the transformation of society's normativity within the morphogenetic interplay between personal reflexivity and Agency.

The internal conversation is viewed as the anchor of personal and socio-cultural morphogenesis. As a result, reflexivity is restricted to personal deliberations as the efficient cause of change. The aim of rethinking the morphogenetic equation is to expand reflexivity beyond the personal while maintaining a stratified conception of personhood. Seeking to ascribe primacy to the interactive dynamics within relations that anchors personal and socio-cultural morphogenesis, the revision of the morphogenetic equation is twofold:

1. The psycho-developmental perspective on personhood distinguishes the different ways the reflexive capacity can be enacted.
2. Reflexivity is extended to social relations and is not exclusive to individuals.

Regarding the first revision, the idea of differentiated developmental selves accounts for the emergence of the reflexive capacity. The developmental focus leads to a view of reflexivity as semantically possible. At the same time, due to the self-presence of experiences, the reflexive capacity is enacted as part of an irreducible developmental trajectory. This irreducibility is affected by pre-existing pre-semantic mechanisms that impact the direction of reflexivity.

Reflexivity, therefore, is a meaning-making mechanism that is not necessarily tied to individuals to safeguard against the sociological imperialism of the conceptual self. Instead, it extends to any activity that shapes morphogenetic outcomes. The management of personal morphogenesis is the task of individuals who exist within a system's interactive dynamics that includes personal, collective, and social reflexivity. The outcomes of these dynamics are seen in the emergent properties that make up the system. Triple morphogenesis, then, is the product of the interactive dynamics between the reflexivity of individuals, collective *Relational Subjects*, and social networks.

Social Capitalisation and the Making of Relational Goods

An immanent critique of social capital theories demonstrates that, due to their individualistic or holistic starting points, analytical closure leads to a conceptual incapability to account for the internal dynamics of social capital's production. The alternative proposed here is that social capitalisation is part of the morphogenetic processes of sociability, the ties of which are expressed within interactions. These interactions, because of their proximity, are sources of social capital; they generate *ASV* that augments the processes of sociability through the generation of primary *relational goods*.

Relational goods, as the effects of sociability, are both dependent and independent variables. In a stratified understanding of social reality, whether *relational goods* explain or are the object of explanation is determined by the temporal stage of a *morphogenetic cycle* under analysis. Social capital as a *relational good* is produced in processes of capitalisation (the generation of *ASV*) that exist within reciprocal interchanges. It enables the development of Alter within the fabric of sociability that is renewed through the continued production of *relational goods*.

The proposal of a morphogenetic *civil society* is based on the dialogue between the processes of sociability and their outcomes that reference the human-in-the-social. Within this dialogue, *civil society* emerges from the reflexive interdependence between different dimensions of sociability that produce *relational goods*. To reiterate, in starting from the relation, the *morphogenetic paradigm* can explain the origins of existing conditions of production and their consequences. The relational ethicality of *civil society* implicates the *meta-reflexive* management of these conditions in the form of synergy between *primary, secondary, and generalised sociability* (the synergy being the mode of production of *relational goods*). Together, these forms of sociability articulate social capitalisation in making *relational goods*. Social capital as a *relational good* is both an outcome and a contributing factor in the morphogenetic process.

A Relational Realist Utilisation of the AGIL Scheme

The AGIL scheme is a compass to understand the relationship between integrative and referential social realities, that is, the recursive relationship between sociability and *relational goods*. When reconsidered through the relational *symbolic code*, it is used to guide a relational ethicality in which *relational goods* are emergent from reciprocal relationships. The integrative reality of AGIL is the socio-cultural structure that relationally guides morphogenetic processes of sociability. In turn, the *relational goods* produced from the interplay between the formal and active inform the future direction of the referential and integrative realities of AGIL.

In the case of education, the formal organisation of networks is the structural aspect of sociability that guides and nurtures the application of the curriculum and assessment within learning environments. What transpires in the classroom utilises relational concepts and practices discovered in dialogue within the interactive dynamics of teaching and learning (the 'black box' of sociability). Reference to these changing concepts and practices is the shifting subjective access points of the learner, that is, the ability to scaffold the learner to the next stage of a learning cycle.

While the learner's changing access points represent the referential reality of education's AGIL, the importance of pre-existing criteria-based goals is necessary as a directive constraint. The dialogical posture of learning, considering the relational nature of cognitive processes, means that the constraint of criteria simultaneously enables personal development. Thus, the student's developmental reality (L) is not externally negated in the organisation of teaching and learning (I). The organisational dimension of AGIL adapts in reference to the way the student develops — a *meta-reflexive* process that is first articulated dialogically by the teacher within the interactive morphogenetic dynamics.

Situated Pedagogy and the Interplay between Direction and Liberation

In a 'directive liberating' approach to education, curriculum design is considered to emerge from the 'black box' of sociability. The curriculum takes different dimensions depending on its role — whether as a primary or secondary relation good. In terms of classroom practice, the lived curriculum is experienced in the context of the student's personal development. The planned curriculum is a secondary *relational good* whose features change based on the dynamics of relations of proximity.

Whether at the level of *generalised sociability* or *primary sociability*, the curriculum is tied to the development of Alter. Assessment evaluates the efficacy of the delivered (planned) curriculum in its capacity to direct the learner. In this context, evaluation enables learning development by scaffolding the learner. Teaching and learning concepts and practices are renewed within school-based environments according to judgements about what works in a student's development. As a result, school-based research merges assessment practices with the development of the learner through *judgemental rationality*. This is a *meta-reflexive* judgement on what works when considering the maximisation of development.

The relational realist approach, in merging assessment with subjective input, contrasts with prevailing methods that start from desired outcomes. Disconnecting outcomes from the individual's starting point in this way leads to evaluations of the delivered curriculum through norm-referenced assessment. In such a scheme, the goal is not to develop the student through the criteria; instead, it uses criteria to assess if students are meeting the selection process of pre-set roles. Accordingly, when starting from the learner's perspective, it is necessary to distinguish between *how* to assess and *what* to assess. The *how* dimension refers to the organisational facet of the AGIL compass, whose design and application are based on Alter's given morphogenetic starting point (L). Therefore, the conceptual outcome sought — *what* to assess — refers to the value pattern of the AGIL scheme due to its reference being a subjective developmental point.

Assessment within teaching and learning relations enables the development of Alter's potentiality. In developing this potentiality, assessment integrates the learner into a subject's criteria self-referentially. The ipsative-referenced dimension of assessment ensures that criteria guide the learner (assessment *for* learning) rather than judge him or her (assessment *of* learning). There is an 'in-gear' conception of freedom in this after-modern context: interaction with a pre-existing world enables the learner's agency, as enacted through the interdependence between control and freedom. The authority of criteria is expressed in a problem-posing dialogical relationship in which learning is co-directed with the teacher. When standards are self-referenced, they are aligned with a subjective access point within teaching and learning situations. Such situated pedagogy means that the status-roles of *Ego and Alter* are constantly changing in response to the dynamics of learning and knowing. Authority — in this situated sense — guides the student to competencies that underpin critical investigation and prolonged study.

Primacy ascribed to the lived and experienced curriculum ensures that development occurs coherently. The curriculum, therefore, is not merely something that establishes what to learn; instead, it sets a blueprint that guides the development of skills necessary to enable self-reliant learning. In the lived and experienced curriculum, the ipsative consideration is expressed in the student's awareness of how to monitor and evaluate self-growth. While one-off norm-referenced assessment produces learner dependency, assessment literacy develops self-reliant learners who continuously observe and evaluate their growth. As assessment practices are intertwined into the lived and experienced curriculum, the delivered (planned) curriculum guides learner agency by harmonising subjective access points (the personal morphogenesis of the learner) to its goals.

Final Comments

The argument presented in this book finds its culmination in how teaching and learning are planned and delivered within the epistemic dialogue between *Ego and Alter*. This dialogical approach opposes the epistemic closure of pre-set learning outcomes and the universal application of grade bands in system-based governance. When the overarching objective is to integrate individuals into collectives, then teaching and learning are tied to standards that define reciprocated expectations between actors. The negation of subjective learning cycles directly follows from making the pre-defined referential axis of the welfare state the starting point of education. Within such meritocratic regimes, discourses of fairness act as an aspect of collective interventions to ensure talent is developed through the provision of system-defined relevant work-based skills.

In opposition to modern *lib/lab* governance, the morphogenetic articulation of relations continuously generates *relational goods* in *civil society*. Whether through the activity of the individual or collective *Relational Subjects*, the generation of *relational goods* leads to the solidarity necessary for creating social capital. *Relational Subjects* become drivers of civil welfare whose activity exists in a broader network-like structure emergent from morphogenetic processes (Donati & Archer 2015).

These morphogenetic processes *meta-reflexively* extend the parameters of sociability based on the emergent goals pursued.

In an after-modern context, solidarity is produced within relations of proximity and is continuously enhanced by primary *relational goods*. The generation of primary *relational goods* is guided by formalised organisational settings whose integrative practices and policies reflect the relations it seeks to regulate, that is, its *symbolic reference*. This way, secondary *relational goods* — the formal organisational settings of networks — are the structural aspect of AGIL that manage differentiation at the intersubjective level. It is the management of differentiation in a relational way (the mode of production) that ensures the patterns of sociability produce *ASV* in exchanges between *Ego and Alter*. In opposition to modernity's functional model of integration, the outcomes produced are a function of the relations between subjects oriented to each other as *Relational Subjects*.

In an educational context, policies and practices may be instituted to enable talent development by creating *relational goods*. To achieve this goal, the curriculum must be both a primary and secondary *relational good* in terms of its temporal place within morphogenetic processes. These processes renew the fabric of sociability and the different dimensions that define it as a relational order. Solidarity is expressed in the engagement of learners in reciprocal (dialogical) relationships with teaching and learning. In such a scheme, education is directed by integrating the learner into an existing body of knowledge through self-referenced developmental milestones. The broader institutional network provides the infrastructure setting that produces the necessary social capital for individuals to pursue personal growth and development. Documentation of learning and the iterative planning of pathways to further learning is part of an educational relational order that ties the curriculum to the ipsative evaluation of talent development.

Talent development should be understood in its broader sense. It is self-referential (ipsative) to ensure developmental coherence and relevance to Alter, but it is also part of a wider *civil society*. *Affective outcomes* include attitudinal changes that develop with the demands of 'rigorous rigour' (Freire in dialogue with Shor 1987b) in learning to participate and to reach a critical judgement. Talent development is identity formation that is relationally constituted, that is, the identity of

Relational Subjects that belongs to others through a logic of non-negation. As part of personal morphogenesis, identity formation is realised via developmental access points. These access points are opportunities for a 'liberatory invitation' that utilises dialogue within teaching and learning relationships to guide students in applying their reflexivity in reference to their relations (Freire in dialogue with Shor 1987b). The 'rigorous rigour' of *relational reflexivity* is part of *affective outcomes* that nurtures a relationality based on a mode of knowing directed at the emergent mediations between *Ego and Alter*.

There is a difference between a dialogue based on individual experiences and one that is part of the process of learning and knowing (Freire in dialogue with Macedo 1995). In the latter, learning and knowing include experiences as part of relations to the world (natural, practical, and discursive) that dialectically facilitate subjectivity's critical relationship to objectivity. The aim is to transcend these experiences through an attitude of epistemological curiosity that referentially detaches from the inhabited world (Freire in dialogue with Shor 1987b). To abstract from the given entails a situated and dialogical pedagogy authentic to Alter's point of development. The authority of constraint mentors Alter into knowing how to know in new ways in the spirit of solidarity. It is only through consideration of the wider socio-cultural context — the organisational dimension of AGIL — that creates the conditions that make a shared and emergent 'We-ness' possible.

Glossary of Key Terms

Added Social Value (ASV) is an emergent effect of personal, collective (agential), and social reflexivity within the interactive dynamics of social bonds. The effect of these dynamics can be witnessed in collective goods that enhance the parameters of sociability by enabling social actors with opportunities and resources to develop their latent potentiality. Relationships between collective goods and the properties of sociability are mediated by the reflexive action of *Relational Subjects*. In the *morphogenetic paradigm*, the relationship between *Relational subjects* and sociability — with *ASV* of collective goods as the product of the relationship — becomes two realities generated and regenerated in different stages of a *morphogenetic cycle* (Donati & Archer 2015).

Civil Society is the expression of a project of 'societal citizenship' (Donati 2021). In this project, *Relational Subjects* are responsible for mediating the processes of sociability in making *relational goods*. The development of positive freedom that enables *Relational Subjects* is part of a mode of production that is built on a co-growth of freedom and control:

> The political expression of this project is 'societal citizenship', intended as citizenship distinct from the governmental sense. Societal citizenship is produced by forms of bottom-up social governance. It is built as a co-growth of freedom and control within a framework of social solidarity, through distance relationships between civil society and the state, rather than as an ascriptive emanation of the nation-state (implemented, as in modernity, through the principle of progressive inclusion of the population in it). (Donati 2021: 43)

Rather than nation-state citizenship, *civil society* is characterised by 'societal citizenship', which is an implication of social governance in which citizens as *Relational Subjects* are relationally reflexive in the mode of production of *relational goods*. The *relational goods* produced establish the identity and direction (control) through which citizens are developed (freedom) to be part of the making of socio-cultural morphogenesis. The democratic character of participation is embedded in the citizen's relationality, ensuring *relational goods* as goods of sociability. As a result, the making of *relational goods* in its participatory mode of production sustains *civil society*.

The **Common good** is relational as it rests on the activity of reciprocally oriented *Relational Subjects*. As a good that rests upon the relations of subjects, it references the common needs of those in relation to one another (the relation's 'We-ness'). The *common good* is different to both the private and public goods that are inherently non-relational in their production and maintenance:

> Saying that a common good is relational means that it is a type of good that depends on the relations of the subjects toward one another and can be enjoyed only if the subjects orient themselves accordingly. In this sense, we say that human life is a common good in that it is the object of enjoyment and therefore of rights, not as a private, individual good in an individualistic sense, nor as a public good in the modern technical sense of a state good, but precisely as a relational good of subjects who are relation with one another. (Archer and Donati 2015: 215–216)

The **DDD scheme** conceptualises lifelong internal conversations in three stages: discernment, deliberation, and dedication:

- Discernment: In the first stage, there is the inner dialogue that reflects on the past and future, considering emergent subjective concerns about the natural, practical and discursive orders. This initial reflection represents the phase of possibility in relation to the concerns faced. The person reflects on current satisfactions and dissatisfactions as he or she registers what is worthy of consideration.

- Deliberation: Deliberation builds upon the initial reflection in the discernment phase, as the person identifies the implications of choosing specific paths. It is in the deliberation stage that previously registered concerns are ranked. Based on this ranking, an envisioned path is drawn as a particular way of life. Often, this phase of the process entails a visual projection of scenarios seeking to capture, as best the subject is able, the *modus vivendi* that would be involved, whilst listening to the emotional commentary that is provoked and evoked when imagining that particular way of life (Archer 2007: 20).

- Dedication: The final phase (stage three) moves from the moment of prioritisation based on the person's ultimate concerns to the decision point. Making decisions is pre-supposed by an inner struggle that leads to a distinct alignment within the person and the emergence of the personal identity.

Cognitive and affective outcomes. Learning outcomes are cognitive and affective. *Cognitive outcomes* refer to the intellective dimension that provides critical capacities in analytical literacy and subject knowledge. Affective outcomes, by contrast, are related to changes in the student's perspective and attitudes — these can include, for example, self-reliance, self-discipline in forming views, and social responsibility. Two data types can be collected when assessing outcomes: behavioural and psychological (Astin & Antonio 2012). Behavioural data consists of observable changes, whereas psychological data seeks to demonstrate internal changes in the student. Nevertheless, both outcomes are interrelated, that is, cognitive changes in knowledge entail affective changes that manifest as personal growth and maturation.

Double contingency. The morphogenetic passage from T1 to T2 represents the point of individual reflexivity concerning the socio-cultural context. In the first stages, dependent on individual deliberation, there is a relation of simple contingency. The movement to the interactional stage T2–T3 introduces a relation of *double contingency* between *Ego and Alter* within wider networks. In this stage, the relationship between *Ego and Alter* is inherently unpredictable as it denotes the dedication of individual reflexivity to the role of Agency, which mediates existing structures with others.

The nature of the existing structure in stage T2–T3 stabilises the contingency of expectations in which reflexivity is enacted. In the logic of non-negation, meta-reflexive management of *double contingency* is achieved by seeking *relational goods* to ensure the increased differentiation at the level of interaction produces structures at stage T4. The result exemplifies adaptive practices and policies of *civil society* that refer to the human/non-human distinction (Donati 2011).

Ego and Alter represent any relationship between self and the other in a social context. As a reciprocal exchange, it refers to the subjective and reflexive side of interaction in gaining knowledge (observation). Operating within a network of relations, *Ego and Alter* include reciprocally oriented agents/actors and social systems/social spheres (Donati 2011).

The reciprocal effect of the relation between *Ego and Alter* produces a reality that exceeds both and is viewed in two dimensions: (1) the *symbolic reference* as *refero*; (2) the structural bond as *religo*. The *refero* is the meaning ascribed to the relation, and the *religo* is the objective ties between *Ego and Alter* shaped by these meanings. In relational realism, these dimensions are interwoven, generating relations (an emergent *generative mechanism*) as *refero* and *religo*. Hence, as a *generative mechanism*, relations have distinct properties and powers.

The **epistemic fallacy** refers to the reduction of being to the mode of knowing. It occurs when the judgement of an object of reference becomes analytically tied to the limitations imposed by the epistemic approach. For example, the genetic fallacy is the imposition of invariants — such as ideas of human nature — on the explanation of contingent historical occurrences. Epistemic and genetic fallacies interrelate when ideas about an invariant (mode of knowing) are used to abstract from complex historical processes (Hartwig 2007). In methodological relationism, disconnected language games are invariants that limit how the external world is understood. The result is a concern with immediacy: we are left with current interactions and the utilisation of practically informed tools to understand those interactions.

In a realist model of causality, a **generative mechanism** is not simply the exercise of powers in observed events. Instead, it is the latent reality of the object (Prandini 2011). The unrealised potential of dormant and unexercised powers is due to the absence of complementary conditions. Accordingly, the development of unrealised powers is the objective of mediations between the first and second triangles of the epistemic quadrangle (see figure one in Chapter Two). As the second triangle refers to the *latent ontological reality*, then reflexive mediations are needed to realise the potential of this latent reality in the context of new morphogenetic patterns of sociability, that is, a broader network of supporting *generative mechanisms*. Importantly, the identity of a relation is not reducible to those directly involved — it is a reality that exceeds the participants and includes a broader environment that directs relationships relationally.

Judgemental rationality is distinguished from judgemental relativism. In the latter case, there is no ground to prefer one view over another. *Judgemental rationality*, however, is pre-supposed by epistemic relativity, in which judgement is historically situated and contingent (Hartwig 2007: 242). As the referent is historically situated and relationally embedded, judgements are likewise grounded in the conditions of its emergence. Nevertheless, as the object is an irreducible determinant of relations, *judgemental rationality* maintains a transcendent dimension to the referent in its potentiality that needs to be discovered. *Judgemental rationality* thus aims to arrive at a better understanding through evolving referential acts that are not relativist in an absolute sense.

The **latent ontological reality** is the potentiality of the object with respect to its conditions of sociability. Potentiality implicates the human's transcendence (the latent) as irreducible to its existing immanence. Consequently, emancipatory social mediations (immanence) should actualise the *in potentia* powers of the human beyond the observed in a particular morphogenetic phase. Meta-reflexive social relations are articulated to draw out the latent reality of the human. This activity generates patterns of sociability capable of relating to and developing the potentiality of the human.

The **lib/lab mode of governance** is grounded in modernity's *symbolic code* of negation. It is based on a functionalist *symbolic reference* that operates through two poles — the free agency of the individual as producer and consumer (lib) and the collective state-defined structures that represent systematic controls to regulate those personal liberties (lab) (Donati 2011: 25). The market pole (lib), with its affirmation of free agency in a productive sense, is the referential dimension of governance — when the state intervenes it seeks to regulate and ensure fairness in the taking up of opportunities in the lib side. Whatever the configuration between lib and lab, the former dictates the terms of reference between *Ego and Alter*. The organisational ties that emerge articulate this referential dimension.

The third way between lib and lab covered in this book is an attempt to create synergy between both poles to ensure that impersonal market forces and interventionist policies can be compatible in fluid circumstances. Individual endeavour is acknowledged with the state intervening to regulate this endeavour by connecting the individual to social mechanisms that provide opportunities. In this policy triangulation, there is an explicit discourse that presents the inadequacy of the lib-dominated policy — where society is predominantly viewed as an aggregate of individuals — and state-driven lab collective interventions that seek holistic outcomes. Nevertheless, regardless of rhetoric, policy triangulation reproduces modernity's *symbolic code* of negation as it views freedom (lib) and control (lab) in a binary way in which the failings in either pole need corrective mechanisms defined by system imperatives that are dictated by impersonal market forces. Limitations on what is possible in mediations between *Ego and Alter* are pre-defined in accordance with external state-defined mediations of relations.

Meta-reflexivity. Archer (2012: 13) identifies four modes of reflexivity: communicative, autonomous, meta-reflexive and fractured. In the communicative mode of reflexivity, 'internal conversations need to be confirmed and completed by others before they lead to action'. By contrast, in the autonomous mode, 'internal conversations are self-contained, leading directly to action'. The meta-reflexive mode of reflexivity is one in which 'internal conversations critically evaluate previous inner dialogues and are critical about effective action in society'. Finally, in fractured reflexivity, internal conversations 'cannot lead to purposeful courses of action, but intensify personal distress and disorientation resulting in expressive action'.

In this book, reflexivity is understood as meaning-based activity. Thus, reflexivity takes a collective dimension to include the actions of collectives (collective reflexivity of Agency) and the internal dynamics of social networks as social reflexivity. *Meta-reflexivity* is the mode of reflexivity of *Relational Subjects* as producers of *relational goods*.

The *morphogenetic paradigm* aims to explain personal and structural change by breaking events into time-bound tractable phases (**morphogenetic cycles**). Whether in the case of the emergence of personal identity or structural elaboration, working between stages T1 to T4 connects forward and backwards-looking cycles. Consequently, a new emergent entity in stage T4, with its distinctive properties and powers, impacts the interactions of the next cycle.

The **morphogenic paradigm** is an explanatory framework that complements and is derived from relational realism. It does not specify which mechanisms are given primacy to dictate the direction of analysis. Consistent with the relational realist paradigm, it takes the relation and its dynamics as its first ontological premise rather than starting from specific mechanisms. Thus, the *morphogenetic paradigm* establishes a guideline to investigate the way outcomes are first anchored in personal morphogenesis in the form of individual deliberation that links the interplay between social agency and the development of socio-cultural structures. Within this interplay, it examines both the transformation (diachronic development) and endurance (synchronic presence) of relational configurations based on the commitment of persons as Corporate Agents whose actions are enacted through time-bound interactions.

A **philosophical ontology** indicates the 'general categorical form of the world' (Hartwig 2007: 178). It is a starting point for the possibility of social scientific investigation, that is, a transcendental perspective about what causes social scientific practice to produce knowledge independent of the observer (Prandini 2011). If practices are to identify what makes the world intelligible or 'real', then an *a priori* framework needs to be proposed to account for this intelligibility. Thus, transcendental realism is about the question of being — it argues that how we relate to the external world impacts the epistemological approach utilised to understand this external world better. In relational realism, the general categorical form of the world is its relationality; as the internal dynamics of the relation is the first ontological principle, concepts and tools developed need to be refined to approach the referent in a responsive socio-cultural context. On the other hand, substantive ontology refers to specific contents of the world that are explained based on a paradigm. As argued in Chapter Two, a substantive theory is necessarily derived from a *philosophical ontology*. The epistemic quadrangle is an example of a general approach from which the *morphogenetic* explanatory paradigm is derived.

Relational goods emerge and are intrinsically defined from the relations between subjects. As *relational goods* depend on the activity of those in relation, they cease to exist without their continuous interventions. The production of *relational goods* through *Relational Subjects* involves interactions that enhance patterns of sociability capable of generating and regenerating *relational goods*. At morphogenetic stage T4, the *relational goods* produced are emergent effects with distinctive properties and powers impacting interactive patterns in the next cycle that regenerate social structures enabling *Relational Subjects* to make further *relational goods*.

Relational goods produced can be deeply intersubjective or formalised and impersonal. In the former case, primary relational goods denote *relational goods* produced by the family and small informal groups. Secondary *relational goods*, on the other hand, are impersonal and have an associational and organisational character (Donati and Archer 2015).

Primary, secondary, and generalised sociability. Sociability refers to orders of social relationality, including interpersonal (informal face-to-face interactions) and impersonal (formal organisations and social movements). The impersonal form of social relationality is an aspect of sociability when actively producing pro-social effects that generate *ASV* necessary to create *relational goods* (Donati & Archer 2015). Based on the distinction between different types of social relationality, sociability consists of primary, secondary, and generalised forms.

Primary sociability refers to informal networks constituted by family and community. *Secondary sociability* refers to formal social networks consisting of organised associations fostering trust and collaboration within a community that is part of a broader *civil society*. Finally, *generalised sociability* is less particularistic in its sphere of focus — it relates to impersonal relations that foster trust towards others outside particular communities (activities of this nature can include the development of the planned curriculum and inter-institutional collaboration rules discussed in Chapter Six). *Generalised sociability* aims to generate an attitude of trust and belonging to a broader social context that includes others outside the particular community or association (Donati & Archer 2015).

There are continuities and interdependencies between these different forms of sociability; they mutually impact each other. Sources of social capital produced in each form of sociability result from this mutual impact that reflexively adapts to deliver effective collective goods. Collective goods are *relational goods* produced in social relationality (personal or impersonal) that enhance the stock of social capital necessary for making future *relational goods* within *morphogenetic cycles*.

Relational reflexivity employs *meta-reflexivity*, which is exerted on the properties and powers of the relationship between *Ego and Alter*. It aims to manage the relationship through the organisational mechanisms that bind participants in reference to an emergent *symbolic reference* (shared identity) that provides a compass to its direction (Donati 2021).

Relational Subjects are central to the activity of mediations at stage T2–T3. As an individual or collective social subject, in *civil society*, the *Relational Subject* is 'relationally constituted' to be reflexive towards the performance of associational networks (stage T2–T3) that make up the outcomes they produce, including social reality. The ensuing *relational reflexivity* is built on the relational constitution of positive freedom manifested in developed emergent properties and powers through working in tandem with others (Alter). The nurturing of positive freedom transforms the socio-cultural contexts and their mode of producing relational goods or evils. In turn, the outcomes produced from the reciprocal exchanges at T2–T3 have properties and powers that impact the identity and direction of the relation that constitutes *Relational Subjects* in future *morphogenetic cycles*. Hence the reciprocal interactions between *Ego and Alter* reference outcomes in the form of the *common good* that represents those involved in its making. The *common good* in the form of *relational goods* represents the 'We-ness' that defines the orientation of social relationality open to transformation through the reflexive activity of *Relational Subjects* that are the engine of social morphogenesis (Donati & Archer 2015).

The **symbolic code** refers to the epistemological framework that underpins the relation's identity, or 'We-ness' (*symbolic reference*). Knowledge generated in mutual interactions is an outcome of how the mediation between *Ego and Alter* is conceived. Modernity's *symbolic code* starts from the premise of negation as relations between distinctions (observer and observed) are governed externally. Consequently, the epistemic outcome and identity of the relation reach a resolution in a binary way. As knowable reality is governed through an oscillation between state and market, the acknowledgement of distinction is de-focused, resulting in an exclusionary formula between Ego (A) and Alter (non-A), that is, [A = non (non-A)]. Policy innovation within such a binary is pre-restricted and operates within the analytical framework of modernity's *symbolic code*; it works between institutional individualism and state-driven interventions to connect individual goals to system needs. Due to the negation of the relationality of social relations, the direct implication of modernity's *symbolic code* is a functionalist logic in which policies conceptually operate in and through pre-existing system needs of *lib/lab governance*.

In contrast, the after-modern *symbolic code* understands knowledge to arise from and through relations. The identity and direction of these relations recognise forms of knowledge to develop from shared mediations that are referentially tied to the human-in-the-social. Consequently, in opposition to modernity's *symbolic code*, the formula that captures the after-modern *symbolic code* is an inclusionary one of non-negation grounded ontologically in the relation between A and non-A, that is, [A = r (A, non-A)] (where r = relation). The relational character of knowledge is the basis of transformative policies and practices that references the relation's distinctions (Donati 2011: 69–70).

The **symbolic reference** is the value base of the relation derived from the *symbolic code* that establishes the epistemic framework of interactive dynamics. For example, if a relational *symbolic code* defines the relationship, the semantic identity between *Ego and Alter* will be based on a dynamic of non-negation. In the case of non-negation, the emergent 'We-ness' is defined from the *relational reflexivity* of *morphogenetic* mediations. The organisational dimension that follows from non-negation is an outcome of morphogenetic processes that direct future mediations. Hence, we have three dimensions to the relation:

1. The *symbolic reference* is the relation's value base that acts as the reference of mediations between *Ego and Alter*.

2. The structural bind that organises the relation between *Ego and Alter* considering the *symbolic reference*.

3. In a *symbolic code* of non-negation, reciprocal action is based on *relational reflexivity* that transforms the *symbolic reference* and its structural bind to meet the needs of the human-in-the-social in a better way.

References

Alderwick, H. (2012) 'Continuity with New Labour? Deconstructing the Triangulation of David Cameron's Conservatives', *POLIS*, 12, pp. 1–49.

Astin, A. (1999) 'Student Involvement: A Developmental Theory for Higher Education', *Journal of College Student Development*, 40(5), pp. 518–529.

Astin, A. (2016) 'Are You Smart Enough?: How Colleges' Obsession with Smartness Shortchanges Students', *Journal of Student Affairs Research and Practice*. Sterling, VA: Stylus Publishing.

Astin, A. and Antonio, A. (2012) *Assessment for Excellence: The Philosophy and Practice of Assessment and Evaluation in Higher Education*. 2nd edn. Washington DC: Rowman & Littlefield Publishers.

Allais, S. (2012) '"Economics Imperialism", Education Policy and Educational Theory', *Journal of Education Policy*, 27(2), pp. 253–274.

Archer, M. (1995) *Realist Social Theory: The Morphogenetic Approach*. Cambridge: Cambridge University Press.

Archer, M. (1998) 'Introduction: Realism in the Social Sciences', in Archer, M. et al. (eds.) *Critical Realism: Essential Readings*. Abingdon: Routledge, pp. 189–205.

Archer, M. (2000) *Being Human: The Problem of Agency*. Cambridge: Cambridge University Press.

Archer, M. (2003) *Structure, Agency and the Internal Conversation*. Cambridge: Cambridge University Press.

Archer, M. (2011) 'Morphogenesis: Realism's Explanatory Framework', in: Maccarini, A.M., Morandi, E., Prandini, R. (eds.), *Sociological Realism*. Abingdon: Routledge, pp. 59–94.

Archer, M. (2012) *The Reflexive Imperative in Late Modernity*. Cambridge: Cambridge University Press.

Archer, T. and Vanderhoven, D. (2010) *Growing and Sustaining Self-Help: Taking Big Society from Word to Action*. Community Development Foundation. Available at: https://www.bl.uk/collection-items/growing-and-sustaining-self-help-taking-the-big-society-from-words-to-action

Ashton, J. (2010) 'Inequalities, assets and local government - opportunities for democratic renewal posed by the global economic crisis', in Campbell, F. (ed.) *The social determinants of health and the role of local government*. London: Local Government: Improvement & Development Agency. Available at: https://www.local.gov.uk/sites/default/files/documents/chapter-10-inequalities-a-6a9.pdf.

Ayers, S., Flinders, M. and Sandford, M. (2018) 'Territory, Power and Statecraft: Understanding English Devolution', *Regional Studies*, 52(6), pp. 853–864.

Ball, S. (2009) 'Privatising Education, Privatising Education Policy, Privatising Educational Research: Network Governance & The "Competition State"', *Journal of Education Policy*, 24(1), pp. 83–99.

Ball, S. and Exley, S. (2010) 'Making Policy with "Good Ideas": Policy Networks and the "Intellectuals" of New Labour', *Journal of Education Policy*, 25(2), pp. 151–169.

Ball, S. and Olmedo, A. (2013) 'Care of the Self, Resistance and Subjectivity Under Neoliberal Governmentalities', *Critical Studies in Education*, 54(1), pp. 85–96.

Bevir, M. (2005) *New Labour: A Critique*. Oxford: Routledge.

Bhaskar, R. (1998) *The Possibility of Naturalism: A Philosophical Critique of the Contemporary Human Sciences*. 3rd edn. London: Routledge.

Bhaskar, R. (2007) 'Theorising Ontology', in Lawson, C., Latsis, J., and Martins, N. (eds.) *Contributions to Social Ontology*. Abingdon: Routledge.

Bhaskar, R. (2008) *A Realist Theory of Science*. Abingdon: Routledge.

Boud, D. and Soler, R. (2016) 'Sustainable Assessment Revisited', *Assessment and Evaluation in Higher Education*, 41(3), pp. 400–413.

Bourdieu, P. (1977) *Outline of a Theory of Practice*. Cambridge: Cambridge University Press.

Bourdieu, P. (1986) 'The Forms of Social Capital', in *Handbook of Theory and Research for the Sociology of Education*. Westport, CT: Greenwood Press, pp. 241–58.

Bourdieu, P. (1990) *The Logic of Practice*. Translated by R. Nice. Stanford: Stanford University Press.

Bourdieu, P. (2000) *Pascalian Meditations*. Stanford: Stanford University Press.

Bourdieu, P. (2008) 'The Left Hand and the Right Hand of the State', *Variant*, 32, pp. 3–5. Available at: https://www.variant.org.uk/pdfs/issue32/Bourdieu32.pdf

Bourdieu, P., Chamboredon, J.-C. and Passeron, J.-C. (1991) *The Craft of Sociology: Epistemological Preliminaries*. Edited by K. Krais. Translated by R. Nice. Berlin: Walter de Gruyter.

Bourdieu, P. and Wacquant, L. J. D. (1992) *An Invitation to Reflexive Sociology.* Cambridge: Polity Press.

Bourdieu, P., Wacquant, L. J. D. and Farage, S. (1994) 'Rethinking the State: Genesis and Structure of the Bureaucratic Field', *Sociological Theory*, 12(1), pp. 1–18.

Bowles, M. (2010) 'The Big Society and the responsive state'. Community Development Foundation. Available at: http://www.oneeastmidlands.org.uk/sites/default/files/library/CDF_expert_panel_paper_two_-_The_Big_Society_and_the_responsive_state%5B1%5D.pdf

Burstow, B. (1991) 'Freirian Codifications and Social Work Education'. *Journal of Social Work Education*, 27, pp. 196–207.

Bruner, J. (1999) *The Process of Education.* Cambridge: Harvard University Press.

Cabinet Office (2010) 'Behavioural Insights Team'. *Applying Behavioural Insight to Health.* London: Cabinet Office Behavioural Insights Team. Available at: http://www.cabinetoffice.gov.uk/sites/default/files/resources/403936_BehaviouralInsight_acc.pdf

Cabinet Office (2011) 'Community Development Foundation to Deliver the £80m Community First Programme'. Available at: https://www.gov.uk/government/news/community-development-foundation-to-deliver-the-80m-community-first-programme

Cabinet Office (2011) 'Behavioural Insights Team'. *Better Choices: Better Deals, Consumers Powering Growth.* Available at: https://assets.publishing.service.gov.uk/government/uploads/system/uploads/attachment_data/file/294798/bis-11-749-better-choices-better-deals-consumers-powering-growth.pdf

Cameron, D. (2011) *PM's speech on Welfare Reform Bill.* Available at: http://www.number10.gov.uk/news/pms-speech-on-welfare-reform-bill/

Cameron, D. (2009a) *A radical power shift*, The Guardian. Available at: http://www.guardian.co.uk/commentisfree/2009/feb/17/cameron-decentralisation-local-government

Cameron, D. (2009b) *David Cameron: The Big Society.* Available at: http://web.archive.org/web/20091113144156/http://www.conservatives.com/News/Speeches/2009/11/David_Cameron_The_Big_Society.aspx

Cameron, D. (2009c) *David Cameron: Jewish Care.* Available at: http://web.archive.org/web/20100402100140/http://www.conservatives.com/News/Speeches/2009/06/David_Cameron_Jewish_Care.aspx

Cameron, D. and Clegg, N. (2010) 'David Cameron and Nick Clegg : We'll Transform Britain by Giving Power Away', *Daily Telegraph.* Available at: http://www.telegraph.co.uk/news/politics/david-cameron/7884681/David-Cameron-and-Nick-Clegg-Well-transform-Britain-by-giving-power-away.html

Cameron, D. and Herbert, N. (2008) 'Unlocking Democracy: 20 Years of Charter 88', in Facey, P., Rigby, B., and Runswick, A. (eds.) *Unlocking Democracy: 20 Years of Charter 88.* London: Politico's Publishing Ltd, pp. 115–125.

Chambers, D. W. (2019) 'Is Freire Incoherent? Reconciling Directiveness and Dialogue in Freirean Pedagogy', *Journal of Philosophy of Education*, 53(1), pp. 21–47.

Colander, D. and Qi Lin Chong, A. (2010) 'The Choice Architecture of Choice Architecture: Toward a Non-Paternalistic Nudge Policy', *Journal of Economic Analysis*, 1(1), pp. 42–48.

Coleman, J. S. (1975) 'Social Structure and a Theory of Action', *The Polish Sociological Bulletin*, (31/32), pp. 19–32.

Coleman, J. S. (1990) *Foundations of Social Theory.* Cambridge: Belknap Press.

Collier, A. (1994) *Critical Realism: An Introduction to Roy Bhaskar's Philosophy.* London: Verso.

Collier, A. (1999) *Being & Worth.* London: Routledge.

Collier, A. (2007) *In Defence of Objectivity & Other Essays: On Realism, Existentialism & Politics.* Abingdon: Routledge.

Community Development Foundation (2010) 'Identities and Social Action: What Does It Mean for the Frontline?' Community Development Foundation. Available at: http://cdfpreview.web.coop/wp-content/uploads/2011/12/Identities-and-social-action-What-does-it-mean-for-the-frontline.pdf (Accessed: 5/11/2015).

Community Development Foundation (2011) *Briefing Paper: Localism Bill.* London: Community Development Foundation. Available at: http://cdfpreview.web.coop/wp-content/uploads/2011/12/Localism-Bill-briefing-external-updated-08.02.11.pdf (Accessed: 5/11/2015).

Connor, S. (2010) 'The Myth of Community?', *Concept: The Journal of Community Education and Practice Theory*, 1(3) Available at: http://concept.lib.ed.ac.uk/article/view/2284/3400

Conservative Party (2009) 'Get Britain Working'. Available at: https://www.conservatives.com/~/media/Files/Policy%20Documents/GetBritainWorking.ashx?dl=true (Accessed: 5/11/2015).

Conservative Party (2010a) 'National Citizen Service'. Available at: https://www.conservatives.com/~/media/Files/Downloadable%20Files/NCSpolicypaper.ashx?dl=true (Accessed: 5/11/2015).

Conservative Party (2010b) 'Big Society, not Big Government'. Available at: https://www.conservatives.com/~/media/Files/Downloadable%20Files/Building-a-Big-Society.ashx (Accessed: 5/11/2015).

Crisp, R. *et al.* (2009) 'Continuity or Change: Considering the Policy Implications of a Conservative Government', *People, Place & Policy Online*, 3(1), pp. 58–74.

Cruickshank, J. (2003) *Realism and Sociology: Anti-Foundationalism, Ontology and Social Research*. London: Routledge.

Cruickshank, J. (2004) 'A Tale of Two Ontologies: An Immanent Critique of Critical Realism', *The Sociological Review*, 52(4), pp. 567–585.

Cruickshank, J. (2007) 'The Usefulness of Fallibilism in Post-Positivist Philosophy: A Popperian Critique of Critical Realism', *Philosophy of the Social Sciences*, 37(3), pp. 263–288.

Cruickshank, J. (2010) 'Knowing Social Reality: A Critique of Bhaskar and Archer's Attempt to Derive a Social Ontology from Lay Knowledge', *Philosophy of the Social Sciences*, 40(4), pp. 752–773.

Cumming, L. (2010) 'To Guide the Human Puppet: Behavioural Economics, Public Policy and Public Service Contracting'. The Serco Institute. Available at: https://www.sercoinstitute.com/research/2010/to-guide-the-human-puppet

Department for Business, Innovation & Skills (BIS) (2014) *British Invention: Global Impact — The Government's Response to Sir Andrew Witty's Review of Universities and Growth*. London: Department for Business, Innovation & Skills (BIS).

Department for Education (2010) 'The Importance of Teaching: The Schools White Paper 2010'. The Stationery Office. Available at: https://www.gov.uk/government/uploads/system/uploads/attachment_data/file/175429/CM-7980.pdf

Department for Education (2019) 'Government Response to the Education Select Committee report: Value for Money in Higher Education'. Department for Education. Available at: https://assets.publishing.service.gov.uk/government/uploads/system/uploads/attachment_data/file/768965/Value_for_Money_in_Higher_Education-Government_Response.pdf

Department for Education (2021) 'Skills for Jobs: Lifelong Learning for Opportunity and Growth'. Department for Education. Available at: https://www.gov.uk/government/publications/skills-for-jobs-lifelong-learning-for-opportunity-and-growth

Department for Education & Skills (2003) *The Future of Higher Education*. London: Department for Education & Skills. Available at: http://www.educationengland.org.uk/documents/pdfs/2003-white-paper-higher-ed.pdf

Department for Education and Employment (1999) *Learning to Succeed: A New Framework for Post-16 Learning*. London: Further Education Development Agency. Available at: https://archive.org/details/learningtosuccee0000grea/mode/2up

Department Of Social Security (1998) *New Ambitions for Our Country: New Contract for Welfare*. London: Stationery Office Books.

Donati, P. (2009a) 'Beyond Multiculturalism: Recognition Through the Relational Reason', *Polish Sociological Review*, 2(166), pp. 147–177.

Donati, P. (2010) 'Reflexivity After Modernity: From the Viewpoint of Relational Sociology', in Archer, M. (ed.) *Conversations About Reflexivity*. Abingdon: Routledge, pp. 144–164.

Donati, P. (2011) *Relational Sociology: A New Paradigm for the Social Sciences*. Abingdon: Routledge.

Donati, P. (2012) 'Beyond the Market/State Binary Code: The Common Good as a Relational Good', in Schlag, M. and Andrés Mercado, J. (eds.) *Free Markets and the Culture of Common Good*. Heidelberg: Springer.

Donati, P. (2013) 'A Multicultural Society Needs a Relational Reason', *Acta Philosophica*, 22(2), pp. 349–360.

Donati, P. (2014) *Transcending Modernity: The Quest for a Relational Society*. Bologna: Cesis-Department of Sociology and Business Law, University of Bologna.

Donati, Pierpaolo. *Transcending Modernity with Relational Thinking*. Abingdon: Routledge, 2021.

Donati, P. and Archer, M. (2015) *The Relational Subject*. Cambridge: Cambridge University Press.

Doughney, J. (2006) 'The No "Ought" from "Is" Argument: Faulty thinking in Ethics and Social Science', *Journal of Business Systems, Governance and Ethics*, 3(1), pp. 27–40.

Driver, S. and Martell, L. (1997) 'New Labour's Communitarianisms', *Critical Social Policy*, 17(52), pp. 27–46.

Evans, S. (2010) 'Mother's Boy': David Cameron and Margaret Thatcher', *British Journal of Politic and International Relations*, 12(3), pp. 325–343.

Exley, S. and Ball, S. (2011) 'Something old, something new... understanding Conservative education policy', in Bochel, H. (ed.) *The Conservative Party and Social Policy*. Bristol: Policy Press, pp. 97–118. Available at: https://academic.oup.com/policy-press-scholarship-online/book/22949/chapter-abstract/183499323?

Fairclough, N. (2000) *New Labour: New Language?* London: Routledge.

Finlayson, A. (2010) 'The Broken Society versus the Social Recession', *Soundings*, 13(44), pp. 22–34.

Franklin, J. (2007) 'Social Capital: Between Harmony and Dissonance'. London: South Bank University. Available at: http://citeseerx.ist.psu.edu/viewdoc/download?doi=10.1.1.116.3282&rep=rep1&type=pdf

Freire, P. (2000) *Pedagogy of the Oppressed*. 3rd edn. New York: Continuum.

Freire, P. and Macedo, D. (1995) 'A Dialogue: Culture, Language, and Race', *Harvard Educational Review*, 65(3), pp. 377–403.

Freire, P. in dialogue with Shor, I. (1987a) *A Pedagogy for Liberation: Dialogue on Transforming Education*. Westport, CT: Bergin & Garvey Publishers.

Freire, P. in dialogue with Shor, I. (1987b) 'What Is the "Dialogical Method" of Teaching?', *Journal of Education*, 169(3), pp. 11–31.

Gallagher, S. and Zahavi, D. (2012) *The Phenomenological Mind*. 2nd edn. Abingdon: Routledge.

Gewirtz, S. et al. (2005) 'The Deployment of Social Capital Theory in Educational Policy and Provision: The Case of Education Action Zones in England', *British Educational Research*, 31(6), pp. 651–673.

Gibson, H. (2015) 'Between the State and the Individual: "Big Society" Communitarianism and English Conservative Rhetoric', *Citizenship, Social and Economics Education*, 14(1), pp. 40–55.

Gleibermann, E. (Not Dated) 'A Pedagogy of Mentoring'. Available at: http://socraticsmentoring.com/wp-content/uploads/2014/02/A-Pedagogy-of-Mentoring.pdf

Hanretty, C. (2021) 'The Pork Barrel Politics of the Towns Fund', *The Political Quarterly*, 92(1), pp. 7–13.

Hartwig, M. (2007) *Dictionary of Critical Realism*. Abingdon: Routledge.

Heppell, T. (2020) 'The Conservative Party and Johnsonian Conservatism', *Political Insight*, 11(2), pp. 15–17.

HM Government (2011) 'Opening Doors, Breaking Barriers: A Strategy for Social Mobility'. Cabinet Office. Available at: https://www.gov.uk/government/uploads/system/uploads/attachment_data/file/61964/opening-doors-breaking-barriers.pdf

Hornby, W. (2003) 'Assessing Using Grade-Related Criteria: A Single Currency for Universities?', *Assessment & Evaluation in Higher Education*, 28(4), pp. 435–454.

Hughes, G. (2014) *Ipsative Assessment: Motivation Through Marking Progress*. London: Palgrave Macmillan.

Jessop, B. (2003) 'From Thatcherism to New Labour: Neoliberalism, Workfarism, and Labour Market Regulation', in *The Political Economy of European Unemployment: European Integration and the Trans-nationalization of the Employment Question*. London: Routledge, pp. 137–153.

Johnson, B. (2019) 'PM statement on priorities for the government: 25 July 2019'. Prime Minister's Office, 10 Downing Street. Available at: https://www.gov.uk/government/speeches/pm-statement-on-priorities-for-the-government-25-july-2019

Johnson, B. (2020a) 'PM's skills speech: 29 September 2020'. Prime Minister's Office, 10 Downing Street. Available at: https://www.gov.uk/government/speeches/pms-skills-speech-29-september-2020

Johnson, B. (2020b) 'PM Economy Speech: 30 June 2020'. Prime Minister's Office, 10 Downing Street. Available at: https://www.gov.uk/government/speeches/pm-economy-speech-30-june-2020

Kaidesoja, T. (2013) *Naturalizing Critical Realist Social Ontology*. Abingdon: Routledge.

Kelly, A.V. (2004) *The Curriculum*. 5th edn. London: Sage.

Kivinen, O. and Piiroinen, T. (2006) 'Toward Pragmatist Methodological Relationalism', *Philosophy of the Social Sciences*, 36(3), pp. 303–329.

Klein, N. (2010) 'Citizen Co-production of Public Services', in. *Andrew Young School of Policy Studies Summer 2010 Internship Program*, Andrew Young School of Policy Studies. Available at: http://aysps.gsu.edu/econ/files/Econ_10_SummerIntern_N.Klein_Paper.pdf (Accessed: 6/11/2015).

Korobkin, R. (2009) 'Libertarian Welfarism', *California Law Review*, 97, pp. 1651–1686.

Labour Party (1997) *1997 Labour Manifesto*. Available at: http://www.labour-party.org.uk/manifestos/1997/1997-labour-manifesto.shtml

Levitas, R. (2005) *The Inclusive Society? Social Exclusion and New Labour*. 2nd edn. London: Palgrave Macmillan.

Levitas, R. (2012) 'The Just's Umbrella: Austerity and the Big Society in Coalition Policy and Beyond', *Critical Social Policy*, 32(2), pp. 320–342.

Lin, N. (2004) *Social Capital: A Theory of Social Structure and Action*. Cambridge: Cambridge University Press.

Lister, R. and Bennet, F. (2010) 'The new "Champion of Progressive Ideals"? Cameron's Conservative Party: Poverty, Family Policy and Welfare Reform', *Renewal*, 1/2(18), pp. 84–109.

Lord Wei (2010) 'Building the Big Society', in. *Big Society Public Services Seminar Series Institute for Government, 6th June 2010*, Cabinet Office. Available at: http://www.instituteforgovernment.org.uk/sites/default/files/Building_the_big_society_lord_wei.pdf

McAnulla, S. (2010) 'Heirs to Blair's 3rd edn Way? David Cameron's Triangulating Conservatism', *British Politics*, 5(2), pp. 286–314.

Mooney, G. and Hancock, L. (2010) 'Poverty Porn and the Broken Society', 39/40, *Variant*, pp. 14–16.

Morrison, D. (2004) 'New Labour, citizenship and the discourse of the Third Way', in *The Third Way and Beyond: Criticisms, Futures and Alternatives*. Manchester: Manchester University Press, pp. 167–185.

Mullainathan, S. and Thaler, R.H. (2000) 'Behavioral Economics'. MIT Dept. of Economics Working Paper No. 00-27. Available at: http://papers.ssrn.com/sol3/papers.cfm?abstract_id=245828

Neisser, U. (1988) 'Five Kinds of Self-Knowledge', *Philosophical Psychology*, 1(1), pp. 35–59.

Newman, J. (2001) *Modernising Governance: New Labour, Policy and Society*. London: Sage.

Page, R.M. (2010) 'David Cameron's Modern Conservative Approach to Poverty and Social Justice: Towards One Nation or Two?', *Journal of Poverty and Social Justice*, 18(2), pp. 147–160.

Parsons, T. (1985) *Talcott Parsons on Institutions and Social Evolution: Selected Writings (Heritage of Sociology Series)*. Chicago: University of Chicago Press.

Parsons, T. (2005) *The Social System*. 2nd edn. London: Routledge.

Paul Johnson, D. (2008) *Contemporary Sociological Theory: An Integrated Multi-Level Approach*. New York: Springer.

Portes, A. (1998) 'Social Capital: Its Origins and Applications in Modern Sociology', *Annual Review of Sociology*, 24, pp. 1–24.

Putnam, R.D. (1995) 'Bowling Alone: America's Declining Social Capital', *Journal of Democracy*, 6(1), pp. 65–78.

Putnam, R.D., Nanetti, R.Y. and Leonardi, R. (1993) *Making Democracy Work: Civic Traditions in Modern Italy*. New Jersey: Princeton University Press.

Reeves, R. (2008) 'This is David Cameron', *Public Policy Research*, 15(2), pp. 63–67.

Reinholz, D. (2016) 'The Assessment Cycle: A Model for Learning through Peer Assessment', *Assessment & Evaluation in Higher Education*, 41(2), pp. 301–315.

Robertson, S. (2010) '"Spatializing" The Sociology of Education: Stand-Points, Entry-Points and Vantage-Points', in *The Routledge International Handbook of the Sociology of Education*. Abingdon: Routledge, pp. 15–26.

Rochat, P. (2010) 'Emerging Self-Concept', in *The Wiley-Blackwell Handbook of Infant Development*. 2nd edn. Chichester: Wiley-Blackwell.

Rodgers, C. (2002) 'Defining Reflection: Another Look at John Dewey and Reflective Thinking', *Teachers College Record*, 104(4), pp. 842–866.

Saltmarsh, S. (2011) 'Economic Subjectivities in Higher Education: Self, Policy and Practice in the Knowledge Economy', *Cultural Studies Review*, 17(2), pp. 115–139.

Sandford, M. (2017) 'Signing Up to Devolution: The Prevalence of Contract Over Governance in English Devolution Policy', *Regional & Federal Studies*, 27(1), pp. 63–82.

Sandford, M. (2019) 'Money Talks: The Finances of English Combined Authorities', *Local Economy: The Journal of the Local Economy Policy Unit*, 34(2), pp. 106–122.

Sandford, M. (2020) 'Conceptualising "Generative Power": Evidence from The City-Regions of England', *Urban Studies*, 57(10), pp. 2098–2114.

Smith, T. (2010) 'The Enabling State', in Shakespeare, T. (ed.) *Small State, Big Society: Essays on Reforming the State to Create a Stronger Economy and Bigger Society*. London: Localis, pp. 43–50. Available at: https://www.localis.org.uk/wp-content/uploads/2010/05/SMALL-STATE-BIG-SOCIETY_FINAL-TEXT.pdf

Sobolewska, M. and Ford, R. (2020) 'Brexit and Britain's Culture Wars', *Political Insight*, 11(1), pp. 4–7.

Social Justice Policy Group (2007) *Breakthrough Britain: Ending the Costs of Social Breakdown*. Centre for Social Justice. Available at: https://www.centreforsocialjustice.org.uk/wp-content/uploads/2018/03/BBChairmansOverview.pdf

Tanner, K. D. (2012) 'Promoting Student Meta-Cognition', *CBE—Life Sciences Education*, 11(2), pp. 113–199.

Thaler, R.H. and Sunstein, C.R. (2003) 'Libertarian Paternalism', *The American Economic Review*, 2(93), pp. 175–179.

Thaler, R.H. and Sunstein, C.R. (2009) *Nudge: Improving Decisions About Health, Wealth, and Happiness*. New Haven, CT: Yale University Press.

Thaler, R.H., Sunstein, C.R. and Balz, J.P. (2010) 'Choice Architecture'. Social Science Research Network. Available at: http://papers.ssrn.com/sol3/papers.cfm?abstract_id=1583509

The Conservative and Unionist Party (2017) 'Forward, Together: Our Plan for a Stronger Britain and a Prosperous Future'. Conservative Party. Available at: https://ucrel.lancs.ac.uk/wmatrix/ukmanifestos2017/localpdf/Conservatives.pdf.

Thrupp, M. and Willmott, R. (2003a) *Educational Management in Managerialist times: Beyond the Textural Apologists*. Maidenhead: Open University Press.

Thrupp, M. and Willmott, R. (2003b) 'The Market, Neo-Liberalism and New Managerialism', in *Educational Management in Managerialist Times*. Maidenhead: Open University Press.

Tomaney, J. and Pike, A. (2020) 'Levelling Up?', *The Political Quarterly*, 91(1), pp. 43–48.

Tomlinson, S. (2003) 'New Labour and EDUCATION', *Children & Society*, 17(3), pp. 195–204.

Tyfield, D. (2007) 'Tracking Down the Transcendental Argument & The Synthetic A Priori: Chasing Fairies or Serious Ontological Business', in

Lawson, C., Latsis, J. S., and Ornelas Martins, N. M. (eds.) *Contributions to Social Ontology*. Abingdon: Routledge, pp. 142–159.

Universities UK and The UK Commission for Employment and Skills (UKCES) (2014) *Forging Futures: Building Higher Level Skills through University and Employer Collaboration*. London: Universities UK & The UK Commission for Employment and Skills. Available at: https://www.gov.uk/government/publications/forging-futures-building-higher-level-skills-through-university-and-employer-collaboration

Van Bouwel, J. (2003) 'When Unveiling the Epistemic Fallacy Ends with Committing the Ontological Fallacy. On the Contribution of Critical Realism to the Social Scientific Explanatory Practice', *Philosophica*, 71, pp. 81–98.

Wells, P. (2010) 'A Nudge One Way, A Nudge the Other: libertarian paternalism as political strategy', *People, Place & Policy Online*, 4/3, pp. 111–118.

Whitaker, G.P. (1980) 'Coproduction: Citizen Participation in Service Delivery', *Public Administration Review*, 40, pp. 240–246.

Williams, B. (2017) 'Theresa May's Premiership: Continuity or Change?', *Political Insight*, 8(1), pp. 10–13.

Williams, B. (2019) 'The Big Society: Ten Years On'. *Political Insight*, 10(4), pp. 22–25.

Williams, J. (2013) *Consuming Higher Education: Why Learning Can't be Bought*. London: Bloomsbury Academic.

Worley, P. (2018) 'Plato, Metacognition and Philosophy in Schools', *Journal of Philosophy in Schools*, 5(1), pp. 76–91.

Wright, A. (2012) 'Fantasies of Empowerment: Mapping Neoliberal Discourse in the Coalition Government's Schools Policy', *Journal of Education Policy*, 27(3), pp. 279–294.

Yancey, K. B. (1998) *Reflection in the Writing Classroom*. Logan, UT: Utah State University Press.

Zahavi, D. (2005) *Subjectivity and Selfhood*. Cambridge: MIT Press.

Zahavi, D. (2009) 'Is the Self a Social Construct?', *Inquiry: An Interdisciplinary Journal of Philosophy*, 52(6), pp. 551–573.

Zahavi, D. (2013) 'Unity of Consciousness and the Problem of Self', in Gallagher, S. (ed.) *The Oxford Handbook of the Self*. Oxford: Oxford University Press, pp. 316–338.

Zahavi, D. and Zahavi, D. (2011) 'The Experiential Self: Objections and Clarifications', in Siderits, M. and Thompson, E. (eds.) *Self, No Self?: Perspectives from Analytical, Phenomenological, and Indian Traditions*. Oxford: Oxford University Press, pp. 56–78.

Zippel, N. (2011) 'Consciousness and Self-Identity', *Philosophy Today*, 55, pp. 143–150.

Index

Added Social Value (ASV) 87, 97, 100–103, 107, 113, 115, 120–121, 139–140, 148, 152, 155, 162

civil society 6–7, 85–88, 100–102, 104, 148, 151–152, 155–157, 162–163

double contingency 53, 55, 157

epistemic fallacy 44–45, 52, 158

generative mechanism 42–43, 53, 59, 158

judgemental rationality 43, 47, 49, 54–58, 101, 145, 150, 159

lib/lab governance 2–3, 5, 12–13, 20–22, 35, 38–41, 105, 107, 112, 144, 151, 159, 164

meta-reflexivity 59, 79–80, 83, 100–102, 104, 113, 116, 119, 136, 146, 148–150, 152, 157, 159–160, 163

outcomes
 affective outcomes 136, 141, 153, 157

cognitive outcomes 136, 141, 157

philosophical ontology 4, 44–46, 49–50, 52, 55, 58, 96, 102, 106, 144, 161

relational reflexivity 4, 81, 86, 122, 153, 155, 163–165

Relational Subject 1, 3–4, 6–7, 12, 54, 86–87, 96–97, 100–104, 113, 115, 122, 129, 139, 145–147, 151–153, 155–156, 160, 162–163, 172

sociability
 generalised sociability 101, 132, 148–149, 162–163
 primary sociability 101, 132, 148–149, 162–163
 secondary sociability 101, 132, 148, 162–163

symbolic code 8, 11, 38–39, 42, 57, 82, 85–86, 96, 107, 111, 113, 116, 119, 144, 148, 159–160, 163–165

symbolic reference 4, 11–12, 100, 105, 115, 144, 152, 158–159, 163–165

About the Team

Alessandra Tosi was the managing editor for this book and performed the copy-editing and proofreading.

Jennifer Moratry proof-read this manuscript. The index was created by Melissa Purkiss.

Jeevanjot Kaur Nagpal designed the cover. The cover was produced in InDesign using the Fontin font.

Cameron Craig typeset the book in InDesign and produced the paperback and hardback editions. The text font is Tex Gyre Pagella; the heading font is Californian FB. He also produced the EPUB, PDF, HTML, and XML editions. The conversion was made with open-source software such as pandoc (https://pandoc.org/), created by John MacFarlane, and other tools freely available on our GitHub page (https://github.com/OpenBookPublishers).

This book has been anonymously peer-reviewed by experts in their field. We thank them for their invaluable help.

This book need not end here...

Share

All our books — including the one you have just read — are free to access online so that students, researchers and members of the public who can't afford a printed edition will have access to the same ideas. This title will be accessed online by hundreds of readers each month across the globe: why not share the link so that someone you know is one of them?

This book and additional content is available at:
https://doi.org/10.11647/OBP.0327

Donate

Open Book Publishers is an award-winning, scholar-led, not-for-profit press making knowledge freely available one book at a time. We don't charge authors to publish with us: instead, our work is supported by our library members and by donations from people who believe that research shouldn't be locked behind paywalls.

Why not join them in freeing knowledge by supporting us:
https://www.openbookpublishers.com/support-us

Follow @OpenBookPublish

Read more at the Open Book Publishers **BLOG**

You may also be interested in:

Daniel A. Wagner, Nathan M. Castillo and Suzanne Grant Lewis (Eds.)
Learning, Marginalization, and Improving the Quality of Education in Low-income Countries
Delivering on the Promise of Democracy

https://doi.org/10.11647/OBP.0256

Patrick Blessinger and TJ Bliss (Eds.)
Open Education: International Perspectives in Higher Education

https://doi.org/10.11647/OBP.0103

Chris Rowell (Ed.)
Social Media in Higher Education: Case Studies, Reflections and Analysis

https://doi.org/10.11647/OBP.0163

www.ingramcontent.com/pod-product-compliance
Lightning Source LLC
Chambersburg PA
CBHW050243170426
43202CB00015B/2902